The Rolando Hinojosa Reader:

Essays Historical and Critical

edited by
José David Saldívar

Arte Público Press
Houston

This volume is made possible through grants from the Texas Commission on the Arts and the National Endowment for the Arts, a Federal Agency.

Arte Público Press
University of Houston
University Park
Houston, Texas 77004

Printed in the United States of America

Revista Chicano-Riqueña
A Review of Hispanic Literature and Art of the USA
Vol. XII Fall-Winter 1984 Nos. 3-4

Publisher: Nicolás Kanellos

Editors: Julián Olivares and José Saldívar

Book Review Editor: Patricia Mosier

Revista Chicano-Riqueña, at the University of Houston, appears quarterly and publishes poetry, fiction, art, plays, essays, articles and reviews. Submissions should be addressed to *Revista Chicano-Riqueña*, University of Houston, University Park, Houston, TX 77004. Submit articles in duplicate with SASE.

Yearly Subscription Rate: individuals, $10; institutions, $15; single copies and back issues, $5.

Revista Chicano-Riqueña is published by Arte Público Press, which is supported in part by the National Endowment for the Arts. This issue has received generous support from the National Endowment for the Arts and the Texas Commission on the Arts. *Revista Chicano-Riqueña* is a member of The Coordinating Council of Literary Magazines.

Revista Chicano-Riqueña is indexed in *Index of American Periodical Verse*, *MLA International Bibliography*, *Chicano Periodical Index*, *Popular Culture Abstracts*, *Hispanic American Periodical Index*, *Sumario Actual de Revistas*.

Acknowledgments

"A Voice of One's Own," by Rolando Hinojosa, was originally presented to the Texas Library Association convention in San Antonio, April 1983.

"The Sense of Place," by Rolando Hinojosa, originally appeared in *The Texas Literary Tradition: Fiction, Folklore, History*, eds. Don Graham, James W. Lee, William T. Pilkington (Austin: The College of Liberal Arts, The University of Texas at Austin and The Texas State Historical Association, 1983), pp. 120-124, as "This Writer's Sense of Place."

"Crossing the Line: The Construction of a Poem," by Rolando Hinojosa, was originally presented to the Department of Chicano Studies' 1980-1981 Colloquy, at the University of Minnesota on October 6, 1980, and later published in the Institute Paper Series of the University of Wisconsin-Milwaukee's Spanish Speaking Outreach Institute.

"Chicano Literature: An American Literature With a Difference," by Rolando Hinojosa, was originally presented at the 1983 CHISPA Conference, Tulane University, New Orleans.

CONTENTS

V. An Interview

Preface

Rolando Hinojosa has become internationally famous as one of the major authors in Chicano literature. His multi-dimensional novel, *Klail City Death Trip* series, marked by an appetite to break out in diverse and conflicting voices and genres, has become the subject of a variety of scholarly investigations and critical commentaries in journals from Havana to Mexico City to Berlin. Yet, although his most acclaimed work, *Klail City y sus alrededores*, winner of the Casa de las Américas Prize (1976), has been translated into German and several sections of the novel have been translated into French, his work has received very little critical attention in the United States. *The Rolando Hinojosa Reader: Essays Historical and Critical*, the first comprehensive analysis of this new segment of American literature, has been produced to fill that void. All of the essays show that Hinojosa's *Klail City Death Trip* series must be understood as different from and in opposition to traditional American literature and ruling culture. And yet, as Hinojosa himself notes in his essay entitled "Chicano Literature: An American Literature With a Difference," Chicano literature must also be understood in its American context, for it takes an oppositional stance deliberately in order to offer its readers a reformulation of historical reality and culture that is more consistent with the way Chicanos actually live in the United States. Because traditional American literature and ruling culture has tried to define the *whole* of American culture, the task of Chicano authors and literary critics has been to re-read our American culture so as to amplify and strategically position the voices of the ruled, exploited, and excluded. Rolando Hinojosa's *Klail City Death Trip* series and our critical interpretation of it, *The Rolando Hinojosa Reader*, thus can be read as part of our ethnopoetic literary process that resists, limits, and alters the cultural domination or hegemony of the ruling culture in the United States. Rolando Hinojosa's opening essays present, in their highly individualized voice, a perfect introduction to the book. The reader not familiar with Rolando Hinojosa's biography, sense of place, and work, will be able to follow the writer's literary and personal trajectory under the author's own careful guidance. I thought it best to present the next three essays according to a generalized pattern that deals with the "totality" of the *Klail City Death Trip* series. The rest of *The Rolando Hinojosa Reader* is comprised of a series of critical examinations of individual books, arranged in the order in which the *Klail City Death Trip* series was originally published. I conclude with an interview with Rolando Hinojosa. Finally, the debt that I—really all of us in Chicano Studies—owe Rolando Hinojosa is incalculable. I hope that what we have written in this book honors what he stands for.

J.D.S.

Rolando Hinojosa
University of Texas at Austin

A Voice of One's Own

I make no claim to a privileged position in regard to living in two cultures or within two cultures or, even, between two cultures. I happen to think and to observe that most of us who reside in Texas live in various cultures, anyway. And, if one is to believe the latest U.S. Census Report in regard to the population make-up of Texas, there are some 2.9 million Texas Mexicans who are residents of this state. Of that number, then, I'd hazard the claim that some ninety-five percent—an arbitrary figure—are bound by both cultures. But, by the same token, and in varying degrees of intensity in acculturation and assimilation, many Anglo Texans and Black Texans are also living in a bicultural environment.

It's a busy two-way street this thoroughfare of ours, and, as is well known, no one group can live and work in proximity to another without developing some cultural as well as some psychological bonds. Now, that some people do not recognize this, or that they choose to ignore this, or that they choose to deny this fact, nevertheless, the fact remains. Eustace Budgell, a minor figure in English history, once remarked that facts are bothersome things in that they refuse to go away. Bonds exist.

The following is a fact of unperceived biculturalism: In this city, the Ignacio Lozano family, through its newspaper, *La Prensa*, and through its other publications as well as through its own publishing house, maintained a Texas Hispanic tradition in arts and letters for over fifty years. And not only here in San Antonio, but also throughout the state. That the majority population, that is, the solely English-speaking population, did not recognize this does not and did not alter the fact that *La Prensa* and thus Texas Mexican letters existed and enjoyed rude health.

That distribution was carried on a daily basis for those fifty years, that Mexican national writers as well as homegrown Texas Mexicans contributed to its literary pages (as my present colleague, Américo Paredes, did, as a young poet some forty years ago) may have been ignored by the rest of Texas, but this too, did not and does not alter the fact of *La Prensa's* long and

11

lively existence.

The inheritors of this half-century of literary tradition were well served by this tradition in Texas, and when their sons and daughters began to write and to publish in Spanish, or in English, or in both languages as a matter of conscious choice, and then began calling it Chicano Literature, it didn't matter if there were denials of its existence—the facts, proofs, and evidence of its existence were and are both palpable and available. And because of subsequent creativity, publication, and distribution, those who buy and read the texts enjoy the two cultures which are, after all, inextricably bound. As professional librarians, I'm sure that you noticed the omission of the words *acquisition* and *cataloguing* when I mentioned creativity, publication, and distribution.

Let me assure you that I and other writers can take care of the first; that friends and colleagues such as Professors Kanellos and Rodríguez* can handle the publication and the distribution of it, but it is you—and no one else—who is responsible for acquisition, cataloguing, and, eventually, the assigning of shelf space for this literature. And this is your charge since one can neither ignore nor deny the existence of this American literature.

All of us live within two cultures—in varying degrees, as I said, and whatever the degree, the two cultures are inescapable.

I speak neither in rancor nor in disappointment; a learned society such as yours needs no preaching of truths since librarians and no one else in or out of the academy are the maintainers and the keepers of the keys to the libraries, those repositories of learning without which no nation can either survive or call itself free. Yours, then, is a most serious responsibility.

When I was first asked to consider speaking before you by Mr. Martínez in the Summer of 1982, I asked him, among other things, what the topic would be. The topic, he said, would be the two cultures. I also took it upon myself that he might have also

*Publisher Nicolás Kanellos and distributor Juan Rodríguez were panelists with Hinojosa at this Texas Library Association session.

meant the lack of awareness and the omissions in Texas' cultures, and I'll tell you why: One of the courses I teach at the University is *Life and Literature of the Southwest*. The number for the course is E 342, an upper division course populated, mostly, by graduating seniors. We read George Sessions Perry, Américo Paredes, Fred Gipson, Katherine Anne Porter, Tomás Rivera, and Larry McMurtry, among others. Prior to my coming to the University on a full-time basis, no Texas Mexican writers were read in that course; it was a simple omission and nothing personal since Texas Mexican writers were already included in similar courses in as disparate universities as Texas A&M, North Texas State University, Tarleton State University, and the like. A simple omission, as I said, and one that was corrected without fanfare.

The chief reason presented for the inclusion of the Texas Mexican writers—and their talent demanded it—lay in the question, how, then, can one conduct classes about Texas literature, in a course devised years ago by J. Frank Dobie, which do not include the writings of and about those Texans who comprise an important part of Texas history and culture? A similar question could be raised for our public and school libraries and their holdings if such omissions exist.

On a personal note, the very fact of my being the issue of my Texas Mexican father and his Anglo Texas wife, and because of my long life in Texas, I have seen and lived in both cultures from a first-hand experience. But it has also been my experience to note a certain reticence by some to recognize the worth of the seemingly parallel cultures in Texas life. As a few of you may know, I was born in the Valley; I was nurtured there and educated there both in Mexican and in American Schools. One language supplanted the other for a while, but eventually they balanced each other out. What developed from this, among other matters, was an idiosyncratic vision of the world; an awareness of differences and similarities. What I worked on, as far as my life was concerned, was toward a personal voice which was to become my public voice.

What you see here, this professor, and what ideas I may present, is what you will see in my writings: the voice doesn't vary—I was not ashamed of my parents after I received my education, for I was not ashamed of them before I acquired one; I never ran out of things to say to them because of my education nor did they to me because of theirs. And neither of them spoke in hushed, soft-Spanish voices as some Chicano writers describe those who speak that often strident and vowel-filled language. In short, they were my parents, and I their son, and I was not going to write about them or about our mutual cultures as if they were pieces of some half-baked mosaic. A mosaic envisioned, and worse, fostered, by some publishing houses which should know better, and do, but who rather choose not to when it comes to selling their books as products and not as conveyors of ideas or truths in respect to this population group.

I come from those cultures, I'm a product—albeit not a finished one, yet—of them, I cannot be anything else, and I choose not to be anything else other than what I am.

At times, I wonder about those who choose adaptation over true happiness in a desire to please others; and I wonder, but not for very long, about those who ignore, and about those who choose to deny the existence of at least two cultures and of the complex symbiotic relationship inherent in the various Texas cultures. It must be a strange world, this ostrich-like existence and attitude which flies—bottoms up, if I may—against evidentiary proof.

When Mr. Martínez invited me to speak on two cultures I was also somewhat befuddled, as no less a figure than Virginia Woolf was befuddled when she was asked to talk on women in literature. In both our cases, there was so much to say and so little time to say it in. Added to this, in her case, she didn't know if she were to be anecdotal about Jane Austen, the Bröntes, Fanny Burney, and Miss Mitford or if she were to talk about women characters in English literature. She decided that what women needed, and lacked, was a room of one's own. And she wrote on that. Recalling that fine introduction of hers to her little book of the same title, I wondered what Mr. Martínez and you had in mind. Was I to be anecdotal? Entertaining? Educational? Or what? As you must know, or suspect, putting oneself in the position of wanting to please the audience is the first step toward abdicating one's position and ideas. I decided that wouldn't do; if I were to accept the invitation, make the time to sit and write an acceptable paper, from my point of view, then I would have to devote the necessary time to think about the vast, the humorous, and the often sad contradictions in Texas; but to embark on that ship and journey lies madness since twenty minutes is hardly the realistic time to list, let alone to comment upon, our shared history and culture. Whatever I did decide, though, it was to be with one's own voice.

What also helped in my decision to accept and to write this paper was that this was not my first talk to librarians on an allied subject: Mexican American literature, which is part and parcel of our Texas culture. Remembering that meeting, I decided to accept the invitation. That talk was given years ago when Mexican American literature was struggling for inclusion in higher education; that time is now past, and now many of us spend time tightening up, shoring up, and continually working up newer themes and topics and dropping others, as one does in the continuous revision of higher education curricula, until the subject is hammered into workable shape. (In a parenthetical remark, I've mentioned the word *decision* no less than half a dozen times here, but you see, it so happens that writing is a decision, and not to be taken lightly).

As to my qualifications to speak on two cultures and on literature of the Southwest, time will take care of that piece of business. Time is the ultimate judge, not I, and not you. Time is also the great leveller, and all of us in this room, myself included, will succumb to time and not all of us in this room will see the end of this century, a mere seventeen-years away. On that somber but realistic note, I'll end my long-winded introduction and begin my brief remarks which deal with my experience as a writer and to personalize my literary career, to quote from the letter of instruction sent by the T.L.A.

I have been writing rather seriously since the age of fifteen, and I had my first acceptance—three of them, in fact—in high school in Mercedes, Texas. It concerned an annual literary event called Creative Bits. These writings were bound and, as far as I know, they were still available some ten years ago, for those curious enough to see them, in the Mercedes High School library.

My first paid publication, on the other hand, appears twenty-seven years later in V. 3, Spring 1972 of the journal *El Grito*. Since then, I've published six books and some sixty plus briefer works of prose, poetry, and assorted critical essays on literature. My publishing career, then, has been brief but feverish.

In my case, it seems that a prolonged drought has been followed by a torrent. I by no means advocate this as a guide for those who wish to write, or, worse still, for those who wish to see their names in print. It just happens to be my case, and since I am unable to alter my life, I accept the way it is turning out. So much, then, for publications.

What do I write about? I write about what I assume other writers write about: that which they know. I happen to know something about people and about how some of us are. I happen to know some history about the Valley, this country, the state. And I happen to work toward improving and maintaining a grip on memory and events. Add to this two lifetimes, one of observation and participation, and another of unsystematic but enjoyable reading, and you'll see that idiosyncratic vision I mentioned earlier, and you'll be able to read the personal and public voices as well as the voices of those hundreds of characters who populate the works: the fair and the mean, the fools and knaves, the heroes and cowards, those who are selfish, and those who are full of self-abnegation in a place called Belken County, of which I'm the sole owner and proprietor, as Faulkner once said when he spoke of his county.

My published career, then, is going on its eleventh year. Because of this, my experiences as a writer are not worth accounting for. It is the time of my childhood and young manhood that have served me well in my writing; that, and a somewhat sketchy education, an interestingly remarkable homelife, and with neither apologies nor bombast, the ability to sit down and write, to rewrite and to keep at it, until I am both satisfied and convinced that nothing more can be added or deleted to whatever it is I'm writing.

These concluding remarks have been mercifully brief for you and me. Thinking back on my life, I found that talking about writing produced very little of it; I decided at one point to cut down on talking and to concentrate on writing. I think it was a wise choice for me.

I am, primarily, a professor of literature, but my writing has increased my capacity for life, and I hope that this has helped my students.

To sum up, I also consider myself a reader and a lover of books; my first school job was that of librarian in the fourth grade in North Ward Elementary in Mercedes; I know the name's been changed, but it will always be North Ward to me. My college job was a four-year stint in the Reserve Reading Room at the University of Texas; I gravitated to those jobs, as you may have already guessed by now, by the example set at home by parents who read to themselves and to each other and who—not once—ever ordered us to read something or—if in the act of reading—not once denigrated the book or the choice of our reading material. I keep reminding myself of this whenever I see my children read whatever it is they read.

In conclusion, I am now convinced that I am a reader who decides to write until the opportunity to read again becomes available.

Rolando Hinojosa
University of Texas at Austin

The Sense of Place

I begin with a quote from a man imprisoned for his participation in the Texas-Santa Fe Expedition of 1841; while in his cell in Mexico City, he spurned Santa Anna's offer of freedom in exchange for renouncing the Republic of Texas. Those words of 1842 were said by a man who had signed the Texas Declaration of Independence and who had served in the Congress of the Republic. Later on, he was to cast a delegate vote for annexation and contributed to the writing of the first state constitution. He would win election to the state legislature and still later he would support secession.

And this is what he said: "I have sworn to be a good Texan; and that I will not forswear. I will die for that which I firmly believe, for I know it is just and right. One life is a small price for a cause so great. As I fought, so shall I be willing to die. I will never forsake Texas and her cause. I am her son."

The words were written by José Antonio Navarro. A Texas historian named James Wilson once wrote that Navarro's name is virtually unknown to Texas school children and, for the most part, unknown to their teachers as well. A lifetime of living in my native land leads me to believe that Professor Wilson is correct in his assessment of the lack of knowledge of this place in which we were born and in which some of us still live.

The year 1983 marks the one hundredth anniversary of the birth of my father, Manuel Guzmán Hinojosa, in the Campacuás Ranch, some three miles north of Mercedes, down in the Valley; his father was born on that ranch as was his father's father. On the maternal side, my mother arrived in the Valley at the age of six-weeks in the year 1887 along with one of the first Anglo-American settlers enticed to the mid-Valley by Jim Wells, one of the early developers on the northern bank. As you may already know, it's no accident that Jim Wells County in South Texas is named for him.

One of the earliest stories I heard about Grandfather Smith was a supposed conversation he held with Lawyer Wells. You are being asked to imagine the month of July in the Valley with no air conditioning in 1887; Wells was extolling the Valley and he said that all it needed was a little water and a few good people. My grandfather replied, "Well, that's all Hell needs, too." The story is apocryphal; it has to be. But living in the Valley, and hearing that type of story laid the foundation for what I later learned was to give me a sense of place. By that I do not mean that I had a feel for the place; no, not at all. I had a sense of it, and by that I mean that I was not learning about the culture of the Valley, but living it, forming part of it, and thus, contributing to it.

But a place is merely that until it is populated, and once populated, the histories of the place and its people begin. For me and mine, history began in 1749 when the first colonists began moving into the southern and northern banks of the Río Grande. That river was not yet a jurisdictional barrier and was not to be until almost one hundred years later; but, by then, the border had its own history, its own culture, and its own sense of place: it was Nuevo Santander, named for old Santander in the Spanish Peninsula.

The last names were similar up and down on both banks of the river, and as second and third cousins were allowed to marry, this further promulgated and propagated blood relationships and that sense of belonging that led the Borderers to label their fellow Mexicans who came from the interior, as *fuereños*, or outsiders; and later, when the people from the North started coming to the Border, these were labeled *gringos*, a word for foreigner, and nothing else, until the *gringo* himself, from all evidence, took the term as a pejorative label.

For me, then, part of a sense of the Border came from sharing: the sharing of names, of places, of a common history, and of belonging to the place; one attended funerals, was taken to cemeteries, and one saw names that corresponded to one's own or to one's friends and neighbors, and relatives.

When I first started to write, and being what we call "empapado," which translates as drenched, imbibed, soaked, or drunk with the place, I had to eschew the romanticism and the senti-mentalism that tend to blind the unwary, that get in the way of truth. It's no great revelation when I say that romanticism and sentimentalism tend to corrupt clear thinking as well. The Bor-der wasn't paradise, and it didn't have to be; but it was more than paradise, it was home (and as Frost once wrote, home, when you have to go there, is the place where they have to take you in).

And the Border was home; and it was also the home of the petty officeholder elected by an uninformed citizenry; a home for bossism, and for old-time smuggling as a way of life for some. But, it also maintained the remains of a social democracy that cried out for independence, for a desire to be left alone, and for the continuance of a sense of community.

The history one learned there was an oral one and somewhat akin to the oral religion brought by the original colonials. Many of my generation were raised with the music written and com-posed by Valley people, and we learned the ballads of the Border little knowing that it was a true native art form. And one was also raised and steeped in the stories and exploits of Juan Nepomu-ceno Cortina, in the nineteenth century, and with stories of the Texas Rangers in that century and of other Ranger stories in this century and then, as always, names, familiar patronymics: Jacinto Treviño, Aniceto Pizaña, the Seditionists of 1915 who had camped in Mercedes, and where my father would take me and show and mark for me the spot where the Seditionists had camped and barbecued their meat half a generation before. These were men of flesh and bone who lived and died there in Mercedes, in the Valley. And then there were the stories of the Revolution of 1910, and of the participation in it for the next ten years off and on by Valley *mexicanos* who fought alongside their south bank relatives, and the stories told to me and to those of my generation by exiles, men and women from Mexico, who earned a living by teaching us school on the northern bank while they bided their time to return to Mexico.

But we didn't return to Mexico; we didn't have to; we were Borderers with a living and unifying culture born of conflict with another culture and this, too, helped to cement further still the knowing exactly where one came from and from whom one was descended.

The language, too, was a unifier and as strong an element as there is in fixing one's sense of place; the language of the Border is a derivative of the Spanish language of Northern Mexico, a language wherein some nouns and other grammatical complements were no longer used in the Spanish Peninsula, but which persisted there; and the more the linguistically uninformed went out of their way to denigrate the language, the stiffer the resistance to maintain it and to nurture it on the northern bank. And the uninformed failed, of course, for theirs was a momentary diversion while one was committed to its preservation; the price that many Texas Mexicans paid for keeping the language and the sense of place has been exorbitant.

As Borderers, the northbank Border Mexican couldn't, to repeat a popular phrase, "go back to where you came from." The Borderer was there and had been before the interlopers; but what of the indigenous population prior to the 1749 settlement? Since Nuevo Santander was never under the presidio system and since its citizens did not build missions that trapped and stultified the indigenous people, they remained there and, in time, settled down or were absorbed by the colonial population and thus the phrase hurled at the Border Mexican "go back to where you came from" was, to use another popular term, "inoperative." And this, too, fostered that sense of place.

For the writer—this writer—a sense of place was not a matter of importance; it became essential. And so much so that my stories are not held together by the *peripeteia* or the plot as much as by *what* the people who populate the stories say and *how* they say it, how they look at the world out and the world in; and the works, then, become studies of perceptions and values and decisions reached by them because of those perceptions and values which in turn were fashioned and forged by the place and its history.

What I am saying here is not to be taken to mean that it is

impossible for a writer to write about a place, its history, and its people, if the writer is not from that particular place; it can be done, and it has been done. What I *am* saying is that I needed a sense of place, and that this helped me no end in the way that, I would say, Américo Paredes in *With His Pistol in His Hand*, McMurtry in *Horseman, Pass By* and Gipson in *Hound Dog Man*, and Owens in that fine, strong *This Stubborn Soil*, and Tomás Rivera in . . . *and the earth did not part* were all helped by a sense of place. And I say this, because to me, these writers and others impart a sense of place and a sense of truth about the place and about the values of that place. It isn't a studied attitude, but rather one of a certain love, to use that phrase, and an understanding for the place that they captured in print for themselves; something that was, for themselves, then, at that time and there. A sense of place, as Newark, New Jersey, is for Phillip Roth, and thus we see him surprised at himself when he tells us he dates a *schicksa*, and then, the wonderful storyteller that he is, he tells us of his Jewish traditions and conflicts, and we note that it becomes a pattern in some of his writings whenever he writes of relationships, which, after all, is what writers usually write about: relationships.

I am not making a medieval pitch for the shoemaker to stick to his last here, but if the writer places a lifetime of living in a work, the writer sometimes finds it difficult to remove the place of provenance from the writings, irrespective of where he situates his stories. That's a strong statement and one which may elicit comment or disagreement, but what spine one has is formed early in life, and it is formed at a specific place; later on when one grows up, one may mythicize, adopt a persona, become an actor, restructure family history, but the original facts of one's formation remain as facts always do.

It's clear, then, that I am not speaking of the formula novel, nor is it my intent to denigrate it or its practitioners; far from it. I consider the formula novel as a fine art, if done well, and many of us know that they do exist. I speak of something else—neither nobler nor better, no—merely different from that genre. It's a personal thing, because I found that after many years of hesitancy, and fits and spurts, and false starts, that despite what education I had acquired, I was still limited in many ways; that whatever I attempted to write, came out false and frail. Now, I know I wanted to write, had to write, was burning to write and all of those things that some writers say to some garden clubs, but the truth and heart of the matter was that I did not know where to begin; and there it was again, that adverb of place, the *where*; and then I got lucky: I decided to write whatever it was I had, in Spanish, and I decided to set it on the border, in the Valley. As reduced as that space was, it too was Texas with all of its contradictions and its often repeated one-sided telling of Texas history. When the characters stayed in the Spanish-speaking milieu or society, the Spanish language worked well, and then it was in the natural order of things that English made its entrance when the characters strayed or found themselves in Anglo institutions; in cases where both cultures would come into contact, both languages were used, and I would employ both, and where one and only one would do, I would follow that as well; what dominated, then, was the place, at first. Later on I discovered that generational and class differences also dictated not only usage but which language as well. From this came the *how* they said *what* they said. As the census rolls filled up in the works, so did some distinguishing features, characteristics, viewpoints, values, decisions, and thus I used the Valley and the Border, and the history and the people. The freedom to do this also led me to use the folklore and the anthropology of the Valley and to use whatever literary form I desired and saw fit to use to tell my stories: dialogs, duologs, monologs, imaginary newspaper clippings, and whatever else I felt would be of use. And it *was* the Valley, but it remained forever Texas. At the same time, I could see this Valley, this border, and I drew a map, and this, too, was another key, and this led to more work and to more characters in that place.

It was a matter of luck in some ways, as I said, but mostly it was the proper historical moment; it came along, and I took what had been there for some time, but which I had not been able to see, since I had not fully developed a sense of place; I had left the Valley for the service, for formal university training, and for a series of very odd jobs, only to return to it in my writing.

I have mentioned values and decisions; as I see them, these are matters inculcated by one's elders first, by one's acquaintances later on, and usually under the influence of one's society which is another way of saying one's place of origin. Genetic structure may enter into holding to certain values and perhaps in the manner of reaching decisions, for all I know. Ortega y Gasset, among others, I suspect, wrote that man makes dozens of decisions every day, and that the process helps man to make and to reach more serious, deliberate, and even important decisions when the time presents itself. A preparatory stage, as it were. The point of this is that my decision to write what I write and where I choose to situate the writing is not based on anything else other than to write about what I know, the place I know, the language used, the values held. When someone mentions universality, I say that what happens to my characters happens to other peoples of the world at given times, and I've no doubt on that score. What has helped me to write has also been a certain amount of questionable self-education, a long and fairly misspent youth in the eyes of some, an acceptance of certain facts and some misrepresentations of the past which I could not change, but which led to a rejection not of those unalterable facts but of hypocrisy and the smugness of the self-satisfied. For this and other personal reasons, humor creeps into my writing once in a while, because it was the use of irony, as many of us know, that allowed the Borderer to survive and to maintain a certain measure of dignity.

Serious writing is deliberate as well as a consequence of an arrived-to decision; what one does with it may be of value or not, but I believe that one's fidelity to history is the first step to fixing a sense of place, whether that place is a worldwide arena or a corner of it, as is mine.

Rolando Hinojosa
University of Texas at Austin

Crossing the Line:
The Construction of a Poem

In the Fall of 1977, my first Fall quarter in Minnesota, I found myself unable to get started on a piece about the Korean War. This was a subject which had been on my mind since the early Spring of that same year, when I had managed to write one brief poem called *Native Son Home From Asia* which the poet Alurista published in his journal, *Maize* (I, 3). But that was all I had managed to set down. I was stuck; there *it* was, and here *I* was with little else to show for it. Still, I thought something was there nibbling and nibbling away, although unable to crack the shell.

I then decided to do what I do best: read. I find that reading solves several problems for me: I'm busy and therefore there's no guilt feeling that comes from inactivity, it also keeps me off the streets, and, as is usually the case, I learn something else about myself. I was sure, I told myself, that something would crop up.

I read some seven or eight histories on the War, and upon finishing them, I discovered to my delight that, invariably, the historians, military and civilians alike, had made shameless use of U.S. Army Public Information releases and other handouts. Among this welter, there was a curious book, a little one, written by a field grade officer in the Indian Army who had been there as an observer. The book concerned itself, primarily, with problems of logistics, and, secondarily, with the tactics and strategy employed by both sides. Also, it did contain a reliable table on chronology. After all of that reading, what I had on my hands were what one would expect: some mental and some handwritten notes that made little sense once removed from the context of the reading.

Now, a writer, this writer, enters easily enough into a state of self-delusion about something being there ready to come out and to be written, but even self-delusion can be carried only so far, and when reality rushes in one has to accept certain facts. One may not wish to believe those facts, but Budgell certainly knew what he was talking about when he wrote that matters of fact are very stubborn things which refuse to go away. In my case, the facts were that, although I may have had something in mind, I had nothing to write about for the time being.

I decided to read some more; I reread all of the *Dance to the Music of Time*, as well as all of Anthony Powell's earlier works; after this, I wrote down some names, but this didn't work, and, added to which, I then had to admit that I had no story to tell. All I had was a suspicion that something was brewing. With that suspicion, and little else, I decided to write some lines in Spanish with an idea of translating them into English. The result of this piece of business was that one set of lines was as bad as the other. In brief, then, five months were spent writing from late Spring to early Fall with precious little to show for it. On the other hand, I was enjoying my classes that fall of '77, exploring the new surroundings in Minnesota, and I was also thinking on the two inches of snow which had fallen in a matter of a few hours on the eighth of October, and, as usual, wondering when I was ever going to write again.

I then took to getting around campus and meeting some of my colleagues in the Departments of English, Spanish and Portuguese, and in the American Studies Program, all within the College of Liberal Arts. This was all very well and to the good, as you may imagine, but the writing wasn't getting done. As I said earlier, Budgell was right: the fact was I couldn't write anything at the time. But writers, if anything, are just as stubborn as facts.

I then read a chapter of a novel I had been working on for some two or three years there; as you can see, I was reduced to reading my own stuff in order to see if there were something there to unlock the dam, open the locks, et-cetera. The section I mention is called *Con el pie en el estribo*, and it appeared in *The Bilingual Review/La Revista Bilingüe* (III, 1). I read it aloud; I then recorded it on a cassette and listened to it. But this too bore no fruit as far as I could tell.

This state of affairs can produce what the late Walt Kelly, the creator of *Pogo*, once called 'the joe blakes'. Now, one of the consequences of the 'joe blakes' is constant worry, another is frustration, and this, at times, can lead to the kicking of otherwise innocent household cats of which we have three. One serious result of cat kicking is that it tends to strain family relations, to say nothing of the cat's feelings and future attitude and relationship.

At this time I should like to confess that I believe in Christmas and in Christmas gifts. A few days before Christmas in that Fall quarter of 1977, a line in English, not in prose exactly, but in rhythm, as an attempt at poetry, came from somewhere: "At Harvey Lann's Hardware Store, Margaret wants to know." It came after some rewriting, but it came, nonetheless. Now, in Spanish prosody, a twelve-syllable verse is the usual line form of the *arte mayor*. The *arte mayor* is an old, reliable eight verse, twelve-syllable form; it was muscled out of Spanish letters at the beginning of the sixteenth century by the newer Italian hepta- and hendecasyllabic lines which had been introduced to the Peninsula, we are told, by Boscán, among others; it is written down that Boscán himself had been introduced to this new rhythm by Andrea Navaggiero, the Italian man of letters and politics. The *arte mayor* didn't die, of course, it was merely laid aside like the fourteen-syllable (Spanish, not French) Alexandrine which the *arte mayor* itself had displaced. Rubén Darío, as we all recognize, was to resuscitate both forms three hundred years later for many of us to enjoy.

So, there it was, that first line: "At Harvey Lann's Hardware Store, Margaret wants to know." Counting syllables as is commonly done in Spanish, and as is also done in some contemporary poetry written in English, I decided to follow Spanish prosody although using the English language. Of more importance to me at that moment, of course, was that I had written something that promised some possibilities. The next line came easily enough; it was in the seven syllabic manner: "Whatever did he mean, Harv?" This was followed by: "When I asked

Rogelio how it was he spoke that Asian tongue" and then: "He replied that it was due to misspent youth."

I then stopped and asked myself the following question: "Who's Harvey?" I then came up with a much better question: "Who's Margaret?" I say a better question because, after all, it was this woman, this Margaret, who wanted to know something, to resolve something. As to the relationship between these two characters, Margaret, to me, obviously enough, I thought, was Harv's wife. This led to at least two more questions: "What about their relationship, and what is it that she wants to know?"

Looking over the first pencil copy I found that it reads like this:

A.

Original and rewrites:

~~Harvey Lann's~~

~~Moody's~~

At Harvey Lann's Hardware Store,

wants to know:

Margaret ~~asks her husband:~~

Whatever did he mean, Harv?

David   Chinese

When I asked ~~Rogelio~~ how it was he spoke ~~that Asian tongue~~

or whatever it is

~~and~~   a product of

~~He~~ replied that it was ~~due to~~ misspent youth.

he

Final version:

At Harvey Lann's Hardware Store, Margaret wants to know:

Whatever did he mean, Harv? When I asked David how it
was
He spoke Chinese
Or whatever it is,
He replied that it was a product of misspent youth.

You probably noticed that Rogelio's name was changed to
David; later on we'll see why and how this came about and what
it led to.

By way of the first of two parenthetical remarks, I should say
that I held on to *Crossing the Line* for over two years before I
finally sent it off to Nicolás Kanellos at the University of Houston; the poem appeared in *Revista Chicano-Riqueña* VII, 4,
p. 6.

The next section was also the result of several rewrites, and it
was here that the words *harmless* and *cheap* appeared, were
stricken, and reappeared only to be written out again; as can be
seen, they finally stuck. It may be that the idea first arose here
with *harmless* and *cheap* for the ironic ending in the poem.
Irony, as is well known, is the one good defense of the defense-
less.

I should now like to mention, briefly, a matter of style. Since
Harvey was now going to participate, through speech, I wanted
his talk, his speech patterns, to sound like *talk*; nothing new in
this, to be sure, but I am sure we'll agree how often some writers
forget to make talk sound like talk:

B.

Original and rewrites:

The

~~That~~ boy's not right in the head, Maggie, that's all.

~~does~~

~~and he's willin'~~   ~~and he comes cheap~~

He's strong enough, ~~all right; but he's off~~

   ~~he's off, but he's harmless, and he does come cheap~~

~~Harmless, but off~~

                      And
                       ∧
~~and he's harmless.~~ ~~And~~ God knows he's willing

                          ~~and~~

         just

      But it happens that he's
                       ∧
~~Don't He's~~ off a bit. ~~but~~ he's harmless . . . Cheap, too
                       ∧
         But

Final version:

The boy's not right in the head, Maggie, that's all.
   He's strong, And God knows he's willing, but it just happens
That he's off a bit. But he's harmless . . . Cheap, too.

   This is an attempt at natural speech, but, at the same time, I
also wanted to have Harvey introduce himself by means of his
own selection of words. What we have here, then, is a broad
brush-stroke description of the boy reduced to his being harmless, cheap, strong, willing, and off a bit, but harmless. This, of
course, is to reassure Margaret that she's safe. And this, as you
can see, is also Harvey's point of view; we still have to hear from
Margaret and from the boy's side of it. Still, it was a description,
and Harvey, at this point, thinks he has answered Margaret's
question to her satisfaction. The chances are very good that you
are way ahead of me here: they're talking at cross purposes, and
you're right.
   I was now in the middle of a poem coming out in English and

using Spanish prosody as I fluctuated between eleven and thirteen syllables to carry it out; sometimes a line of seven syllables would be followed by a line of five or, to break the monotony that could set in, a long verse of fourteen would be followed by another long verse and thus allow the work itself to find its proper rhythm as I chose one word or this word over another or that one and so on. A poem written in English using Spanish syllabic norms.

Partially satisfied with the first rewrite of that first part which introduces the characters, Margaret's question was still unresolved, and I wasn't sure as to who these people were. The last thing I wanted was to allow the reader to be kept completely in the dark. This is an important consideration; of equal importance was that the way the poem was laid out so far, the piece itself cried out for more information: "Who are these people?"

Obviously, I thought, the time had come to somehow round out the Lanns and the young man:

C.

Original and rewrites:

crossed over

Harvey's a shade over fifty; Margaret has ~~just arrived~~,

and it's Saturday nights for them, usually.

Yes, Margaret has just arrived at fifty and

    though

and she's sending signals to Harv

finds herself

~~but~~ he's not catching, so Margaret slams drawers full of nails

a bit ~~louder~~ than necessary

firmer

She also

                s   during

~~Margaret~~ wondered through the day

and through most of the night,

      ~~was is~~

what it is to make love to a someone who's not quite

      ~~it~~

right in the head;

to

~~To~~ someone who says 'misspent youth' ~~and 'unconventional as it may seem'~~

and, 'you're in great shape Margaret-girl'

When Harvey's not around

~~and~~

Final version:

Harvey's a shade over fifty; Margaret has just crossed the line,
And now it's down to occasional Saturday nights for them.
Yes Margaret has just arrived at fifty, and though
She's sending signals to Harv,
He's not catching. So,
Margaret finds herself slamming drawers a bit firmer than
necessary.
She also wonders during the day and through the night,
What it would be like,
As she says,
To make love with someone who's not quite right in the head:
With someone who says, 'Misspent youth' and,
When Harv's not around: 'You're in great shape, Margaret-
girl.'

From this we now know of Margaret and Harvey and something about the boy as well as some actions on the part of all three. Margaret's frustration is taken out on the nail drawers, but it would have defeated the tone of the poem to have stated that she was frustrated, since it is recognized that it is far better to show than to tell; and, I prefer to show through those slight gestures or movements, those telltale actions that reveal some inner secret. She's had the occasional Saturday nights, and, just perhaps, she's up to here with Harv, with the hardware store, with having reached fifty. Actually speaking, Margaret has gone through two-thirds of her life already, but has she lived them? Her original question is no longer "Whatever did he mean, Harv?" which, one, is perhaps a half-hearted attempt at confessing that she's noticing the boy, and, two, that Harv is not—has not, continues not—to look at *her*. Something, then, has to happen. The writer has stepped in and promised something, now he has to deliver.

It did not escape me that the characterization was schematic, but I decided that it was enough for now and it was there for us to see: the couple's middle age, their marriage life partially gone to seed, their indifferent sex life, from Margaret's point of view, and a hint of those broad-shouldered little slabs Frost wrote about, as well as the additional information that 1) she daydreams about the boy, and 2) that the boy (harmless as he may seem) is a bit of a predator, and he may know more than he allows. This section also develops and moves the poem along; it informs the reader some more by pointing to Margaret's humanity, to let the reader focus a sympathetic—perhaps an understanding—eye upon Margaret standing there with all that hardware looking gloomily and unhappily at the half-century mark. And then there's the repetition of time that runs across the sense of need, of urgency on Margaret's part.

There's more, of course, the hidden rhyme of *though* and *so*, and *night/like/quite/right*, and the alliterative */she's sending signals/* and then */during the day/through the night/* which help in keeping a light tone to the poem. There will be no blood spilled, or so one feels from the poem's tone and rhythm.

I was now at the halfway point and as usual trying to follow Emerson's precept of "the force of few words". I was determined to tell the story in as few words as possible with the thought of adding strength through brevity, taking care not to be too brief and too obscure, but then not giving the game away either.

At this time, I should add, I was still bothered by Rogelio's identity; I couldn't imagine his demeanor, his face, or his height. For some reason I decided to name him David; I have several characters named David; one of them is David *el tío* who was killed in Korea. This new David turned out to be David Ruiz—Sonny, also a Korean War veteran who had apppeared briefly somewhere else. And here's the second parenthetical remark: the Korean theme was dying very hard, and later on in *Korean Love Songs* he was to play an important part.

Well now, I had a Korean War veteran on my hands, and to use a term from The Great War, one who was shell-shocked. This condition may be inferred from Harvey's comment that "the boy's not right in the head." But was he not right in the head? We've seen that the boy takes care to see that Harv's not around when he says what he says to Margaret. For him to say those things could lead one to believe that if Margaret does not encourage him, she neither dissuades nor discourages him, it would seem.

D.

Original and rewrites:

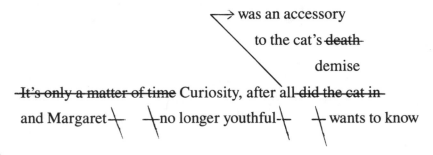

It's only a matter of time Curiosity, after all did the cat in

and Margaret / / no longer youthful / / wants to know

Wants to know

For Herself.

    h

  David   there placed

~~Rogelio~~, Harv wants those kegs nearer the door.

When that's done, I'll give you a glass of ice-cold lemonade.

It's a   ~~really~~
^
~~A~~ substitute that neither one wants

But arranging these things takes time

~~Takes time,~~

                             has
                             ^
and time is something Margaret ~~doesn't have~~

And, yet, doesn't have.

It'll have to be next week, then.

                      at the general meeting of the

Harv'll be ~~gone to the~~ Belken County Hardware
Distributors Association,

And

~~&~~ I'll have myself a headache, she says.

And she does.

Curiosity doesn't always win ~~out~~, and thus the cat survives,

     ~~thus~~

~~and the cat need not die;~~

In time,

~~and so,~~ the drawer slamming stops,

           Saturday

She passes on the nights

~~The Saturdays~~   ~~pass,~~

                                        he's
                                         ↓
and Harv has no complaints about the boy; ~~who's~~ strong,
he works hard

   ~~he~~   and, ~~he comes~~

~~and works hard~~ ~~Cheap, too. And cheap enough.~~

~~most of all, he's harmless & reliable.~~   Cheap, too.

                        ↱
                      ⌐he's reliable.

Final version:

Curiosity, after all, was an accessory to the cat's demise,
and Margaret, no longer youthful,
Wants to know,
for herself.

David, Harv wants those kegs there placed nearer the door.
When that's done, I'll give you a glass of ice-cold lemonade.

It's a substitute that neither one wants, but arranging these things
Takes time, and time is something that Margaret has
And, yet, doesn't have. It'll have to be next week, then.

Harv'll be at the General Meeting of the Belken County
Hardware Distributors,
And I'll have myself a headache, she says.

And she does.

Curiosity doesn't always win, and thus the cat survives.
In time, the drawer slamming stops,
She passes on the occasional Saturday nights,
and Harv has no complaints about the boy; he's strong, he

works hard,
And he's reliable.
Cheap, too.

On the mechanical side of this piece, again, one can see that the various rewritings affected and produced any number of idiomatic, rhythmic, and syntactical changes.

The tone, a light one, had to be maintained, and the idiosyncratic vision had to be maintained also in order not to jar the reader with any unnecessary surprises.

In regard to Margaret, she is Margaret Lann, a character in a poem and she's rather like many men and women who consider themselves attractive and who wish to be, to remain, sexually active, and failing that, to be noticed. To be seen. Not to be taken for granted; another piece of hardware, as it were. Margaret is very human: she's susceptible to flattery. She's fighting the inevitable pull of gravity that will weigh all of us down to the grave. She is what most of us are: ordinarily and extraordinarily human.

Harv is another matter; he's the proprietor of a small business, a husband, a taxpayer like the rest of us, but he is also something else that many of us are not: he's a cuckold. He isn't a ridiculous figure and no evidence is given that he's foolish. What he is, then, is there, much like David is there. Being there, for some things in life, may mean sadness or pleasure by accident of circumstance, may mean glory or ignominy through unknown, or, at times, through mistaken actions, and so forth. We know nothing of the other Harvey Lann, the one he knows, but then he's not under scrutiny here; it's Margaret we're after, and it won't do to dilute a short piece by having too many people in it.

As for David, again, he was there. An object much like the nail drawers, close at hand; an object to be used, and who was used; not necessarily seduced nor the seducer, but used all the same.

In short, what happened to those three in the brief encounter has occurred in many lives throughout history as to be extraordinarily common, that is to say, commonly human.

It's a brief piece, *Crossing the Line*, and it isn't—wasn't—meant to be more than that. What it did for me, however, was to begin the writing of *Korean Love Songs* which had been waiting to come in or to get out, depending on one's point of view. *Crossing the Line* led to David, who then led to *Korean Love Songs*, which then led to *Mi querido Rafa (Dear Rafe)*, a novel in two parts; the first an epistolary and the second, a reportage. But that's another story.

Rolando Hinojosa
University of Texas at Austin

Chicano Literature:
An American Literature With a Difference

Contemporary Chicano Literature may be subdivided into several categories: that one written in English, the one written in Spanish, and, in some cases, the one employing both languages. Further subdivisions could be the urban versus the rural setting or that which presents the cultural nationalistic point of view, and so forth.

I think it is clear that few existing United States literatures present much of a language choice. American Literature, on the other hand, does present language choices; by American literature, then, I mean, as José Martí did, the Americas, meaning the whole of the Western Hemisphere.

Much of the early work of Chicano literature, as well as the contemporary one of twenty years back, was utilitarian, particularly the poetry and, in some cases, the shorter prose. By utilitarian I choose to mean that which was at once didactic to those in the culture — for its reaffirmative or reassuring stance — and to those outside the culture as a means of explication as to who these Spanish-speaking or Bilingual/Bicultural Americans were about. It is now obvious that conflicting and often contradictory messages were being sent out to both cultures.

One example of conflicting reports should suffice for now and should also open up certain areas of discussion: in the early days, invariably, almost every writer claimed to be bearer of the Chicano word.

I'll now touch briefly on the academy and the dissemination of the literature. United States Mexicans, to use that as a conventional term, were publishing and writing many years prior to the Civil Rights Movements of the Sixties. These same Sixties also saw the rise of other ethnopoetic literatures: the Asian-American, the Native-American, and an increased awareness and productivity of the established Black-American Literature. The Sixties also witnessed the birth of Quinto Sol Publications, a publishing house started by a group of junior professors and students at the University of California at Berkeley. The advent of Quinto Sol in an academic center proved to be the germination of later University-based publishers, and thus one saw the rise of the *Revista Chicano Riqueña,* first at Indiana University and now at the University of Houston; the Bilingual Review Press at York College first and later on at Eastern Michigan University, and now at SUNY-Binghamton; *Maize* at the University of California at San Diego, and other publication endeavors as well. Some of the rewards of this early academic setting, by the way, have been the recent publications on Chicano Literature by the University of Texas Press, an extensive bibliography published by the Chicano Center at U.C. Berkeley, and now a recently published history of the literature in the Twayne series. Without going into some of the obvious merits and demerits of the works themselves, this American literature can be judged to be not only surviving here and there, but thriving as well because of increased publications and academic support.

Another of its distinguishing characteristics, or differences, at this stage, is the international recognition it has received in the span of a few years. Improved communications between peoples may be one factor of its recognizability; its quality may be another. In the academy, one of the differences is that this literature is read in Departments of English, Spanish, American Studies, and in the other humanities and social sciences. During the academic revolution of the Sixties when stultified curricula underwent radical changes, Chicano Literature happened to arrive at the precise historical moment for inclusion in the various curricula.

Given the usual in-fighting that we've all experienced in our various disciplines, the inclusion of Chicano Literature was not an easy process, as one can imagine, and it shouldn't have been easy. It was right that it be questioned and tested, that it be examined and held under some very bright lights, and it couldn't and shouldn't have been done in any other way, if it were to survive.

This said, I'll now follow with a necessary digression: One need not go more than thirty years in this country, 1953, say, to prove my following point: I invite everyone to look to your own MLA bibliographies for the number of bibliographical entries for Hispanic American Literature for those times. It was not until 1957 when the National Defense Education Act was proposed and later enacted that Hispanic American Literature came into its own in this country. Mexicanists and other Hispanic Americanists enjoyed, if that's the word, a minority status in the old Romance Language Departments, until they claimed the larger number of graduate students as time went on in the 60's and 70's — yesterday, as it were. It is safe to say that those active 1980's Hispanic American scholars are, for the most part, post 1956-60 Ph.D.s.

So much, then, for tradition in the curricula.

And here's another contradiction: Chicano Literature, which at times passed itself off as a people's literature, was really a child, is actually a child of us, the academicians who make up one of the last of the privileged classes in our native land. (I say privileged because we are deferred to due to our expertise in some instances and because we have the time for reflection; as is often the case, many of us also have time for academic mischief, but that's another story).

I'll now touch briefly on the readership and on the birth of this contemporary American Literature. I'll begin with the second. Since, for the most part, the University was its pediatric ward, a certain stability for the continuance of its reading was insured, much like — and this will hit close to home — much like the continuance of other literatures is insured when taught at the academy. I'll explain by asking two questions: How many volumes of Chaucer and Mío Cid, of Shakespeare and Cervantes, of Pérez Galdós and Hardy would be read in the fifty States semester after semester, quarter after quarter, were it not for all of us who attempt to teach them to our undergraduate students? We contribute to some of their understanding, of course, but we also subsidize these fine authors. How many volumes would be published to be bought and read by the general public? The same can be asked of Chicano Literature, but the difference is the following: countless conversations with students and colleagues at numerous conferences reveal that Chicano students do not, as a rule, sell their literature books back to the bookstore; instead, they take them home to their parents and relatives. And thus it is they who propagate the literature. I have no idea how long the practice will continue, but if it goes on, it points to a further cementing of the literature and its academic base. Now, in the 1980's, there are increasing instances of second and third generation United States Mexican students at the universities; these students avail themselves of the various Chicano offerings and they enroll in these classes as a matter of course; their parents did not because they could not, but now they too enjoy the books.

The wide range of usage and readership may not increase sales dramatically, but when Rivera's . . . *and the earth did not part* or my *Klail City Death Trip Series,* for two examples, are used in courses in Psychology, Social Work, History, Sociology, Education, and in the various literature courses mentioned, this, among other things, means that this fiction has as wide an application as it possibly can in terms of versatility and utility. In some ways, then, it is a people's literature.

There are, then, historical reasons for this phenomenon; for now, one need not go farther back than the Sixties and the already mentioned Civil Rights Movements. It happens, however, that the literature had existed before that time. Much of it was ready to come out as a result of encouragement, in some cases, but also because it was its time to come out then. And come out it did. Since the base was an academic one, book titles were needed and the majority population publishing houses attempted to meet the sudden demand. One of the consequences of this demand in this newly discovered market was the publication and dissemination of some mediocre material; but, mediocre or not, a void needed to be filled and soon there was a union of convenience. As you can certainly imagine, much of this welter fell by the wayside; not all of it, no, and not immediately either, no, but time is a great leveller, and a lot of that early literature sank without a trace, and no great loss, I say.

But time also brings new developments, and in time, other writers began to write and to publish here in this country and abroad. The difference this time was that this American literature was being read in Spanish here and in Spanish-speaking America and, as in any other literature, in translation in various European countries.

It's strange, and perhaps it is far more accurate to say different than strange, when one considers the exportation of a United States literature in a language other than English, and this is what happened to this literature.

Time — again and as always — will be the ultimate judge. And time will also be the witness when one language eventually overwhelms the other in Chicano Literature. With increased urbanization and changes in the culture, English may win out as the dominant language, but there is no guarantee that I'll be proven correct in this regard. The Spanish language, as any other language, may undergo certain linguistic changes, and thus both languages may continue side by side; one never knows.

In closing, I'll say that when Alvar Núñez made his trip from Florida to Texas in the 16th century, he was somehow laying the foundation of a future American literature written in Spanish, north of the Río Grande. As the saying goes, "uno nunca sabe para quién trabaja" and this literature written by United States Mexicans is a constant reminder of a Spanish presence here, in what most of us, I dare say, can legally call our native land. Chicano Literature is a United States literature, but it is also a literature of the Americas, as Martí so clearly saw and labelled the New World.

José David Saldívar
University of Houston

Rolando Hinojosa's *Klail City Death Trip*:
A Critical Introduction

No Chicano writer has been more visibly engaged in the cultural activities of Texas, the Southwest, and *Our* America — to use José Martí's phrase — than Rolando Hinojosa. He has remained actively committed to the literary developments of American ethnopoetics during the past fifteen years, thus becoming in the eyes of many the foremost exponent of Chicano literature. Indeed, Hinojosa's novel, *Klail City Death Trip*,[1] is a sensitive and skillful literary metahistory of the Río Grande Valley, one of the more important dialogical[2] productions of narrative in the Southwest today. It can be safely said that for the general public Rolando Hinojosa represents more an artistic role than an ideological role. But he is, I believe, an important sociopoetic American writer, "looking at the society in general and making telling comments about it as times and the society change in Belken."[3] In this essay, I will reconstruct briefly the evolution of Hinojosa's professional career and the emergence of his "total" literary project.

I.

In a famous essay on the making of the psychoanalytic and Marxist human subject, Fredric Jameson says the following on the function of biographical criticism: "it should be observed that, where the older biographical criticism understood the author's life as a context, or as a cause, as that which could explain the text, the newer kind understands that 'life,' or rather its reconstruction, precisely as one further text in its turn, a text on the level with the other literary texts of the writer in question and susceptible of forming a larger corpus of study with them."[4] I am interested in Jameson's sense of the nature of biography in this section of my study; for Rolando Hinojosa's reconstructed life can serve as a socially symbolic sign, a parallel text of the evolution of his literary project.

Rolando Hinojosa was born in Mercedes, Texas, on January

21, 1929. On his father's side, he is a descendant of the Escandón colonists who came to the Río Grande Valley in the 1740s. On his mother's side, he is a descendant of one of the first Anglo-American families of settlers that arrived in South Texas in 1887.[5]

He attended the Mexican "escuelas" and the American public schools in Mercedes, and at the age of fifteen discovered his literary talent: two of his impressionistic essays on life in his Valley town won a writing contest conducted by his high school teachers. According to the author, the essays are archived in the Mercedes library. Before receiving his undergraduate training at The University of Texas at Austin, Rolando Hinojosa, at the age of seventeen, entered the U.S. Army, completing his tour of duty with the rank of Sergeant. He then continued his studies at The University of Texas. The Korean War, however, interrupted his studies, and he reentered the U.S. Army.

After the war, he returned to The University of Texas at Austin, and he received his B.S. degree in Spanish Literature, with a minor in History, in 1954. He taught at Brownsville High School, from 1954 to 1956, serving as an instructor in Spanish, U.S. Government, and World History. Although his special commitment during these years was to secondary education, his more important decision was to begin a career as a writer. To find more time for his creative writing, he left Brownsville High School to work as a data processor for a chemical company. Although he returned briefly to the classroom in Brownsville, he, once and for all, left secondary education to work as a civil servant for the Social Security Administration. He received an honorable discharge from the U.S. Army Reserve in 1962, with the rank of Lieutenant.

At the urgings of a friend, Rolando Hinojosa entered graduate school at New Mexico Highlands University in 1962, and he received his M.A. degree in Spanish Literature in 1963, compiling an annotation of apothegms, maxims, and proverbs in Cervantes' *Don Quijote*. He continued his graduate studies at the University of Illinois in 1963, where he met formally and informally with Professor Luis Leal for literary discussion. He received his Ph.D. in Spanish Literature in 1969, completing a dissertation on Pérez Galdós entitled *Money in the Novels of Galdós.* He taught at Trinity University in San Antonio, serving as an Assistant Professor (1968-1970).

Rolando Hinojosa moved to Texas A&I University in 1970 as an Associate Professor of Spanish, and Chair of the Modern Language Department. There he taught undergraduate courses in Spanish literature, and he began to publish his short prose pieces about the Río Grande Valley. His first paid publication, "Por esas cosas que pasan," and his ironic *Mexican American Devil's Dictionary I,* a parody of all things political in South Texas, both appeared in *El Grito* (1971 and 1972). *Estampas del valle y otras obras* (1973), his first novel, was awarded the Third Annual Premio Quinto Sol.

In 1974 he was promoted to Professor and selected as the Dean of College of Arts & Sciences at Texas A&I University. From 1974 to 1976, his writing career blossomed, for a number of his Valley fictions appeared in the following Chicano and Hispanic journals: *Caracol, Hispamérica, Mester, Revista Chicano-Riqueña,* and *The Bilingual Review.* As Bruce-Novoa said, "At first glance (these short stories) seemed to be continuations of *Estampas* both in form and content, but no one expected that the next book would bring even higher honors to Hinojosa."[6] Indeed, in 1976 the Latin American judges Juan Carlos Onetti (Uruguay), Domingo Milani (Venezuela), Lisandro Otero (Cuba), and Lincoln Silva (Paraguay) awarded Hinojosa's second novel, *Klail City y sus alrededores,* the highly coveted Casa de las Américas Prize for the best Latin American novel. *Klail City y sus alrededores* was praised for its (post) modernist dialectical forms and content, its artistic use of the revolutionary avant-garde form, collage, its folkloric motifs, and its multiplicity of socio-linguistic dialogues. Almost immediately, Hinojosa's ethnopoetic American subject, Belken County, in general, and Klail City, Texas, in particular, became internationally significant.[7]

In 1976 Rolando Hinojosa was promoted to Vice-President of Academic Affairs at Texas A&I University. His wife, Patricia, however, decided to enter law school, and he accepted an appointment as Professor of English (Creative Writing) and Chair of the Program in Chicano Studies at the University of Minnesota (1976). In Minnesota he wrote *Korean Love Songs* (1978), a book of poems written in the tradition of British World War I poetry. *Korean Love Songs,* as the author remarked in a recent interview, "used poetry to render something as brutal as war,"[8] and expanded the *Klail City Death Trip* series in new ways by foregrounding death and loss as the main project motifs in the novel.

Rolando Hinojosa came to The University of Texas at Austin in 1981 as Professor of English. He is responsible for offering undergraduate and graduate courses in Chicano Literature, Literature of the Southwest, and in Creative Writing. After his return to Texas, he published *Mi querido Rafa* (1981), and in 1982 his epistolary novel was awarded the Southwestern Conference on Latin American Studies Prize for Best Writing in the Humanities. In 1982, he published *Rites and Witnesses,* and later he published *The Valley* (1983), a re-casting and recreation in English of *Estampas del valle y otras obras.* Rolando Hinojosa was inducted into the Texas Institute of Letters in 1983.

With the publication of *Klail City und Umgebung* (Berlin, 1980), a translation of *Klail City y sus alrededores* into German by Yolanda Julia Broyles, and the publication of a large section of *Klail City y sus alrededores* in a new French anthology of Latin American literature entitled *Anthologie de la Nouvelle Hispano Americaine* (Paris, 1983), and the forthcoming publications of *Claros varones de Belken* (Bilingual Press) and *Dear Rafe* and *Partners in Crime: A Rafe Buenrostro Mystery* (Arte Público Press, 1985), Hinojosa's role as the leader of Chicano literature will be firmly established. In brief, though the combination of these multifarious roles — teacher, novelist-essayist-critic — is typical of engaged Third World American intellectuals, what is significant in Rolando Hinojosa's case is his concerted effort to integrate them all.

II.

"I write about Belken County (a fictional county in South Texas) and its people . . . who knows them as well as I do?" — Rolando Hinojosa, from *Chicano Authors* by Bruce-Novoa

Because Hinojosa's fictional world of Belken County has taken shape gradually, critics and scholars have been slow in realizing that an analysis of his work should not only include critical interpretations of individual texts, but also consideration of the whole corpus of the *Klail City Death Trip* series, owing to recurrent characters, scenes, retelling of historical events, and repetition of themes. Because of limited space, I will only offer here a précis of Hinojosa's fictional design; my introductory essay does not pretend to be exhaustive, for a "total" reading of *Klail City Death Trip* would necessarily involve at least three concentric frameworks corresponding to distinct moments in the interpretive process: 1) political history — *KCDT* is made of events, of which one is the appearance of the individual work; 2) society — *KCDT* is characterized by class conflict, and the critic here must catalog the "ideologemes" of our essentially antagonistic collective discourses of social classes; and 3) *KCDT* is to be defined on a materialist basis, that is to say, as a mode of production. The textual dimension of *KCDT* is manifested as the ideology of form.[9]

As it stands, *Klail City Death Trip* is both integrated and disintegrated. Each narrative participates in composing an integrative work at the same time it works out its own individual detachment from it.

In the Caribbean Third World tradition of José Martí's "Nuestra América," the Texas-Mexican literary tradition of Américo Paredes' "*With His Pistol in His Hand,*" and in the traditions of the disintegrating Americas of Faulkner and García Márquez, Hinojosa's *Klail City Death Trip*, through its doctrine of "the political unconscious,"[10] counters historical amnesia by restoring to the materiality of its signifiers that buried reality of South Texas history. As the author said in one of his numerous essays about his "sense of place," "For me and mine, history began in 1749 when the first colonists began moving into the southern and northern banks of the Río Grande. That river was not yet a jurisdictional barrier and was not to be until almost 100 years later; but, by then, the border had its own history, its own culture, and its own sense of place: it was Nuevo Santander, named for old Santander in the Spanish Peninsula."[11] Structurally, it can be safely said that *Klail City Death Trip* is a multi-dimensional, historical novel: it is first an ascent, insofar as the Texas Mexican community struggles, lives, and survives in a segregated society;[12] and second, it is a descent from its Nuevo Santander past, insofar as the old and new guard Texas Mexican Borderers grow more alienated and marginalized by a reifying Texas world. This profound alienation is discernible in many sections of *Klail City Death Trip,* but is especially dramatized in a moving short story entitled "Con el pie en el estribo," where Esteban Echevarría, one of the principal characters of *KCDT,* confides the following to Rafa Buenrostro, one of the novel's principal narrators: "Casa sin corredores, calles sin faroles, amigos que mueren, jóvenes que ya no hablan español ni saben saludar . . . ¡Heh! desaparece el Valle. . . . Los bolillos con sus propiedades, sus bancos y contratos. . . ¿Pa' qué le sirve a uno vivir ochenta y tres años si todo lo que uno vio nacer está enterrado? ¿Los Vilches? ¡Muertos! ¿Los Tuero? ¡También! Los Buenrostro se acaban y las familias fundadoras se secan como las hojas del mesquite doliente."[13] ("Homes without corridors, darkened streets, friends who have passed away, and young people who can't speak Spanish and have no manners . . . ¡Heh! The Valley is gone, people . . . The Gringos got their properties, their banks and contracts . . . What's the use of me living 83 years if everything I grew up with is dead and buried. . . . The Vilches? Dead! The Tueros? They're dead too! The Buenrostros are dying out and the founding families are shriveling up like the leaves of a diseased mesquite tree.") Echevarría's task here, and throughout the *KCDT* series is, I believe, to restructure the problems of ideology, of the unconscious, of desire, and of cultural production around the process of oral narrative. Like Faulkner's and García Márquez's characters, Hinojosa's Echevarría indulges in an ideological nostalgia for an idyllic past where "ese Río Grande . . . era para beber y no pa' detener los de un lado contra el otro," ("that Río Grande was there to provide us with water, not as a fence to separate one from the other"), and where Texas Mexicans defended their homes, families, and communities, with pistol in hand, if necessary. In other words, many of Hinojosa's old guard Texas Mexicans want to stop the clock of time, or regard with pessimistic resignation a degenerating way of life in which people seem helpless to control their fate. Thus, thematically, tradition in the past versus "reification" in the present and future is a basic idea of Hinojosa's *Klail City Death Trip.*[14]

Stylistically, Hinojosa uses his dialogical imagination throughout the project to depict a changing historical materialism in South Texas. His numerous characters reveal themselves to us through what Mikhail M. Bakhtin called "heteroglossia," that is, discourses peculiar to a variety of stratum of society.[15] Indeed, Hinojosa employs a multiplicity of characters and storytellers, making many of them recurring personae, because he wants to resist monologism on the one hand and closure on the other. It should be stressed that *Klail City Death Trip* is not a novel whose essence lies in its plot. ("My stories," Hinojosa remarked, "are not held together by the *peripeteia,* or plot, as much as by *what* the people who populate the stories say and *how* they say it. . . .")[16] But there are countless dramatic incidents, unexpected changes of direction in peoples' lives, and revelations of further depths in character.

Hinojosa's first published novel, *Estampas del valle y otras obras,* in retrospect appears to be the first sketch of his larger masterwork *Klail City Death Trip.* In this book appeared elements which were to recur in nearly all of his later work — Klail

City, a fictional town in the Río Grande Valley, in the midst of a larger North American *société de consommation,* political and racial feuds that (inter)marriages and barbecues cannot heal, and the Valley borderlands themselves which become objects of material desire and social struggle.

Structurally, *Estampas del valle y otras obras* is comprised of four discontinuous parts: twenty portraits of the Valley and its people by Jehú Malacara; six documents describing Baldemar Cordero's fatal stabbing of Ernesto Tamez; a chronicle of brave, craven, loyal, and treacherous Texas Mexicans; and Rafa Buenrostro's remembrances of his primary and secondary school days, and of the Korean War.

As in most of his texts, Hinojosa gives us a fleeting perspective of his characters' lives; Braulio Tapia, Evaristo Garrido, and don Manuel Guzmán, for example, like Echevarría, are connected by the author to the specific Border history of Mexico and South Texas: "Estos viejitos . . . nacieron en (los) Estados Unidos pero guerrearon en la Revolución igual que tantos otros de la misma camada y calaña, como se dice. Los padres de esta gente también nacieron en este país así como los abuelos (aquí se habla ya de 1765 y antes)." ("These old men. . . were born in the U.S. but fought in the Revolution as so many others of the same age and breed. The parents of these men were also born in this country as were their grandparents (and here we are referring to 1765 and before)," *Estampas,* p. l05). Again and again in *Estampas del valle y otras obras,* an historical materialism is dramatized, and the land-grabbing by both unscrupulous Anglos and Mexicans (emblematized in the *KCDT* series by the Leguizamón family) is spelled out: "Los primeros Leguizamón llegaron a Belken County en 1865, después de atole, como quien dice, y se asentaron en lo que son ahora Bascom y parte de Flora. . . . Los primeros Leguizamón supieron defenderse solos a puro pulso contra la bolillada que vino al Valle con la biblia en una mano y el garrote en la otra. . . . En esos tiempos Javier Leguizamón pertenecía al bando de la raza que se granjeaba con los bolillos. Tuvo buenos resultados, recibió bastante tierra en la punta oeste del condado." ("The first Leguizamón arrived in Belken County after 1865; after all had been said and done with, as they say. Some wound up in what is now called the town of Bascom, and others settled near Flora. . . . The first Leguizamón were tough enough to hold on against the Southern Anglos many of whom came to the Valley holding a Bible in one hand and a gun in the other. . . . At that time, Javier Leguizamón belonged to a small group of Mexicanos who sided with the Anglo Texans. His early profits amounted to a fair sized chunk of western county land," *Estampas,* pp. 111-112). It was this technique of uncovering the political, socio-economic, and historical unconscious of the Río Grande Valley which was to inform almost every line of the *KCDT* series.

Klail City y sus alrededores, the next sociopoetic and aesthetic development in the *KCDT* series, can, more than any other of Hinojosa's works, be read independently, and it is his most finished piece of fiction. Perhaps because of this, *Klail City y sus alrededores* is a compendium of the formal and ideological achievements that the author discovered in the creative illuminations of *Estampas* and that he would relentlessly pursue throughout his early literary career. It is a virtual textbook of ethnopoetic and folkloric techniques,[17] one that displays all of Hinojosa's literary talents as the text drives itself to the limits of (post)modernist narrative form: collage and metafiction. *Klail City y sus alrededores* is, in short, another beginning for Hinojosa's great unfinished discourse on the prolonged racism and segregated society of South Texas.

Add to all of this Hinojosa's well-known rhetoric — its mix of wit, "el choteo," and pathos, its oral expansiveness and its dialogic novelistic form — and one can begin to understand what makes his narrative stand out. In his ironic and hyperbolic prologue to this novel, for instance, the narrator tells us, "El número de bolillos que se ven en estos escritos es bien poco. Los bolillos están, como quien dice, al margen de estos sucesos." ("The number of Texas Anglos which appear in these writings is relatively small. The Texas Anglos are, so to speak, marginal to these events," *Klail City y sus alrededores,* p. 11). Given our knowledge of the history of South Texas — the domination of Texas ⸱   ver Texas Mexicans — , we are in a position to detec   ever the text appears to offer judgments with whic   not concur. Thus, from the very start, situationa   irony are going to be the author's favorite trope   *v sus alrededores.*

K   *alrededores* is obsessively concerned with the pro   r, with disjunctive class/race relationships between Texas Mexicans and Texas Anglos.[18] At extremity, Esteban Echevarría's tales at El Oasis cantina (what Mikhail M. Bakhtin would certainly call a "chronotopic" patriarchal center in the novel, "where the knots of narrative are tied and untied")[19] lead to one of the text's most socially symbolic sections — "Echevarría tiene la palabra" — and to the central focus of the novel: the uses and abuses of power in South Texas. Echevarría's listeners at the cantina, are, in effect, a composite of the (phallocentric) audiences Hinojosa visualized as his readers. Through the presence of Echevarría's companions at the cantina, a friendly commerce of oral storyteller and listening group is restored. An intimacy of communication, Echevarría's living voice, and the setting which awakens it, profoundly affects the atmosphere of *Klail City y sus alrededores.*[20]

In "Echevarría tiene la palabra," for example, we learn the following about the insensitive and mendacious ex-Texas Ranger, Choche Markham, and the bitter rivalry between the Buenrostro and Leguizamón families:

> Amigo de la raza, ¡ya quisieran, raza! Choche Markham es bolillo y rinche. . . . La bolillada se cree que los rinches son gallones; me cago en los rinches y en sus pinches fundas contoy pistolas. ¡. . . A ver! ¿Qué le pasó hace unos diez-quince años? ¿Ehm? Cabrón se quiso meter en el asunto aquel de los Buenrostro y los Leguizamón. . . . Cabrón vino echando madres y diciendo que él iba a arreglar a la raza y todo el pedorrón. Pura madre. Los Leguizamón

mataron a don Jesús mientras dormía y ¿qué hizo Choche Markham — les pregunto, raza? — . . . Pos ya saben: no hizo nada. No hizo una chingada. . . ¿Y por qué? . . . (N)o lo hizo por miedo de ir solo y por los favores que le debía a los Leguizamón.

(A friend of mexicanos? Not quite. Choche Markham is a Texas Anglo and a Ranger. . . . All the Texas Anglos think the rinches are hot shit. Let me tell you: the whole mess of them and their guns and holsters too are full of shit. Shit hooks, that's what they are. . . . Let's see. Look at what happened ten-fifteen years ago. Ehm? The son-of-a-bitch said he was going to straighten out the Buenrostro-Leguizamón affair. . . . Son-of-a-bitch raised hell and bragged about straightening us out. Bullshit. The Leguizamóns still went right out and killed don Jesús while he slept and what did Choche Markham do? I ask you, what did he do? — . . . Well you know what he did. Nothing. Not one fucking thing. . . . And why not? . . . Because he was afraid to go by himself and because the Leguizamóns own him, *Klail City y sus alrededores,* pp. 18-20).

Just as Américo Paredes was right on target in his debunking the sacrosanct Texas Ranger mythology in his book, *"With His Pistol in His Hand": A Border Ballad and its Hero,* so Hinojosa's deconstruction of the "rinche" mystique, emblematized by Choche Markham, is so flawless here that the effect is incandescent. *Klail City y sus alrededores'* form and content, its craft and its materiality, like Echevarría's tales themselves, are working in a dialectical accord, at once engagingly distinct and emotionally inseparable.

Hinojosa remarked that he wrote *Klail City y sus alrededores* in order to keep the memory of his youth alive. *Klail City,* indeed, searches for the aura of the past through its adroit use of at least four generations of storytellers, of whom Echevarría, Jehú Malacara, Rafa Buenrostro, and Aureliano Mora are exemplary. For instance, in Aureliano Mora's confession to don

Manuel Guzmán, Hinojosa articulates one of the underlying themes of *Klail City y sus alrededores* and of the entire *KCDT* series: "Es que somos griegos, don Manuel. Griegos en casa de romanos. . . . tenemos que educar a los romanos . . . los bolillos . . . que son lo mismo. . . . Somos griegos, don Manuel, y el día vendrá cuando la raza vive en el condado de Belken como lo hacía antes de que llegaran estos desgraciados." ("We're Greeks, don Manuel. Greeks in the land of the Romans. . . . We have to educate the Romans . . . the Texas Anglos . . . they're one and the same. . . . We're Greeks, don Manuel, and the day will come when Mexicanos will live in Belken County like they did before these wretched Texas Anglos came here," *Klail City y sus alrededores,* p. 137). Hinojosa's critical commentary is, to be sure, heavy-handed here, but Mora, over eighty years old, spells out clearly for us a common belief held by many old guard Mexicanos of the Río Grande Valley: Texas Mexicans are a conquered people economically forced to serve the high barbarism of the conquerors.

As such, *Klail City y sus alrededores* projects a world of tragic realism in which the ultimate entanglements of alienation and desire are so anguished so as to appear almost beyond salvation. Hinojosa's development of what can only be described as "the political unconscious" of South Texas, however, becomes powerful, moving, and brilliant in its scandalous historicizing of the Texas Mexicans' psyche, the self, and senses.

Korean Love Songs, one of the least studied books of the *KCDT* series, gives us a remarkable account of a fragmented, personal, and complex hierarchy — Army life during the Korean War. It gives us Rafa Buenrostro's entirely honest thoughts about that experience. Writing the book in the tradition of British World War I poetry, the author unites a tragic surrealism and an exalted romanticism in such a way that one cannot separate them: each depends on the other for its expression. That is why *Korean Love Songs* is one of the more significant attempts by a Chicano author to record, in all its brutality, a modern technological war. When Rafa Buenrostro, for example, is about to return to Klail City, "That slice of hell, heaven/ Purgatory and land of our Fathers," he writes:

> . . . I'm through here, and I'm through with skull in place.
> In time, the U.S. Army will tell us how many men
> It lost here; for now
> I'll tell you how many friends I lost:
> Chale Villalón and Pepe Vielma,
> Cayo Díaz and a kid named Balderas . . . (*Korean Love Songs*, p.53).

Hinojosa's poetry is not intended for an elite audience. There is a simplicity in these lines memorializing the hundreds of human beings undocumented in our history. With the deaths of friends like Chale, Pepe, and Cayo, Rafa Buenrostro returns home, like many American G.I.s before him, to a changing, modern (reified) Texas society, where Echevarría's idyllic world is dying, "like the leaves of a diseased mesquite tree."

If *Klail City Death Trip* is, in fact, a metahistory of the Río Grande Valley, that is, a fictional text with a deep historical, structural, poetic and sociolinguistic content,[21] then the author's use of language should necessarily register the transitory linguistic changes for the Texas Mexican and Texas Anglo communities. Hinojosa's project, I believe, succeeds admirably in representing the Río Grande Valley's linguistic evolution by dramatizing the range of verbal contacts in South Texas. The following passage is exemplary of Hinojosa's historical project: "El campaign manager raza de Ira, need I say it? es none other than Polín Tapia. Pasó por el banco esta a.m. Picking up orders from Noddy & some dinero; . . . Los años no pasan por ese hombre — ni las indirectas tampoco, pero eso es harina de otro costal. Una vez, allá cuando tú y yo tendríamos unos doce años, Bobby Campbell me preguntó: Is Polín Tapia the mayor of Mexican town?" *(Mi querido Rafa,* p. 29).

Mi querido Rafa, Hinojosa's explicitly bilingual novel, is written in two parts. The first half of this epistolary book contains twenty-two letters written by Jehú Malacara to his cousin Rafa Buenrostro, who is recovering from his war wounds at the Veteran's Hospital in William Barrett, Texas. In these bilingual letters, Jehú Malacara, now an aspiring loan officer at the Klail City Savings and Loan, tells Rafa about the local gossip and reports on his boss's (Albert 'Noddy' Perkins) manipulation of the Klail City elections.

For the first time in the *KCDT* series, we are taken to the very source of financial power in South Texas: the Klail-Blanchard-Cooke capitalists. As an employee of the KBC family's Savings and Loan, Jehú's letters give us insight into how the ruling class uses and abuses the lower classes in South Texas — the Texas Mexicans who make up the great bulk of the poor. We also learn much about Noddy Perkins, his daughter, Sammy Jo, and of Jehú himself. Although Jehú is fired and then rehired by Noddy Perkins, he eventually decides on his own volition to leave his banking job and the Valley for Austin and the university.

The second half of *Mi querido Rafa* consists of a series of interviews conducted by the local Valley writer, P. Galindo. Both Texas Anglos and Texas Mexicans are asked by Galindo what they think of Jehú Malacara's sudden departure from Klail City, for one, it is assumed, does not simply walk away from an important banking job in South Texas in the 1950s. Throughout this half of the novel, P. Galindo remains neutral about Jehú's life and career as a banker, insisting that he opines nothing.

Rites and Witnesses, the latest published book in the *KCDT* series, fills in the gaps *Mi querido Rafa* left open: the 1959-1960 world of Klail City, and the 1950 world of the Korean War. Like Hinojosa's previous texts, this book is a collection of vignettes, dialogues, and reportages about Chicano life in and beyond the Río Grande Valley. In the first part of the novel, entitled "The Rites," Hinojosa describes the gulf of death that Chicanos and other young men entered in Korea. Many of those killed in action, the narrators tell us, had obscure burials, no formal rites or formal ostentation. In the second half of the novel, called

"The Witnesses," Hinojosa juxtaposes the camaraderie that existed among all the soldiers in Korea to the blatant feelings of white supremacy in the Valley, of which the following testimonial by Earl Bennet is representative: "The trouble with Mexicans is that if we give 'em a raise, they'll either get lazy or they'll quit on you; just like that. Looky here: they make as much as they want, and if we step in and give them some more, why, they'll just blow it away. You know, they 'git drunk' and play them some rancheras on that juke box there and adiós mi dinero boys. And that's no lie: I know what I'm talking about" (*Rites and Witnesses*, p. 72). Unlike Hinojosa's earlier books, *Rites and Witnesses* is written entirely in English, reflecting the fact that Jehú Malacara and Rafa Buenrostro are now participating fully in the Texas Anglo world. As the author said in a 1983 interview, "In the first two or three works I focus mainly on the Texas Mexican. But as both Rafe Buenrostro and Jehú Malacara grow up and go into the Army, the University of Texas and the workplace, they're coming into the Texas Anglo world."[22]

Finally, Hinojosa's novel, *Partners in Crime: A Rafe Buenrostro Mystery* (Arte Público Press, 1985), deserves some comment here because in this new novel we can sense the full emergence of a mass-cultural discourse — a first-rate murder mystery — but juxtaposed with it, the full blossoming of the author's radical critique of late capitalism.[23] *Partners in Crime,* set in Klail City, Texas, Barrones, Tamaulipas, and to a lesser extent, Jonesville-on-the-River, Texas, describes a brutal murder and then a group "matanza" (massacre) in October 1972, and Rafe Buenrostro's role in solving the murders of two Mexican nationals, César Becerra and Andrés Cavazos de León, and a Texas Anglo, Gus Elder. The conventional patterns and motifs of the genre are all here in *Partners in Crime*: shrewd detectives (a Texas Mexican, a Texas Anglo, and a Mexican), naive disciples, the "who's next" series, and the misleading direction of genuine clues. Hinojosa's sleuths are Lt. Rafe Buenrostro of the Belken County Homicide Squad and Captain Lisandro Goméz Solís, Cuerpo de Policía Estatal, Sección del Orden Público of

Barrones, Tamaulipas. An unnamed narrator tells the story, and his curiosity and growing awareness of the complexity of the murders underscores Hinojosa's concern with truth and falsity. When the mystery is finally solved by Rafe Buenrostro, we are given a clear message: beware of meaning.

As Hinojosa has done throughout the *KCDT* series, *Partners in Crime* continues to focus on the lives of Rafe Buenrostro and Jehú Malacara who are now in their late thirties. What is especially valuable about *Partners in Crime* is that we learn of significant, but previously unmentioned, details about our protagonists' past. We discover, for example, that Rafe Buenrostro, after his junior year at The University of Texas at Austin, decided to enter law school at UT. He borrowed money from his brothers, Aaron and Israel, to study for the bar exam, passed it, and then, to everyone's dismay, decided to become a Belken County policeman. We also learn that Jehú Malacara, who had resigned as a Loan Officer at the Klail City Savings and Loan and had gone to Austin, had in fact attended graduate school at UT. He dropped out three years later, and has now returned to Klail City and has been rehired by Albert 'Noddy' Perkins as Vice President and Cashier of the Klail City First National Bank.

Whereas in the earlier *KCDT* books, Mexican oil and Valley cotton had generated revenue for the Klail-Blanchard-Cooke family's bank to control and manipulate, in the 1972 world of *Partners in Crime,* multi-national "racketeers" are forcing their way into the Belken County economy — what Noddy Perkins reads as "someone trying to fiddle with our money." Hinojosa's project motif of death and loss is dramatized in *Partners in Crime* by the use value and exchange value of marijuana and cocaine; their transformation of the Valley economy; their fragmentation of the family unit (working class and bourgeois); and their disruption of traditional values. Throughout this fast-paced novel, Hinojosa's study of perceptions and ideology of South Texas is at its sharpest, for the communal world forged by Guzmán, Mora, and Echevarría, and the bourgeois-capitalist world produced by the Klail-Blanchard-Cooke family, has been displaced by the world-market of racketeering, the author's critical metaphor of late capitalism and the end of reason in South Texas.

In sum, with the same effect as the traditional historical novel,[24] Hinojosa's *Klail City Death Trip* invents a body of characters and discourses in which we see reflected the ways of a South Texas society and the people who constitute it. In few ethnopoetic American novels do we find so many characters whose changing fate and self-revelation we follow through so many years and with such extraordinary vicissitudes. Rafa Buenrostro, Esteban Echevarría, Jehú Malacara, Albert and Sammy Jo Perkins, Choche Markham, Polín Tapia, Lisandro Gómez Solís, Irene Parra — these are figures whose histories of personal, collective, and social destiny prove unforgettable. And there are literally hundreds of other characters, most of whom one cannot even mention in a short introductory study like this, but most of them recurring across the pages of *Klail City Death Trip,* found there in new situations and offering further insights into their nature and their history.

[1]*Klail City Death Trip,* the project title of Rolando Hinojosa's work, is comprised of the following books: *Estampas del valle y otras obras* (Berkeley: Quinto Sol Publications, 1973), *Klail City y sus alrededores* (Havana, Cuba: Casa de las Américas, 1976); subsequently published in a bilingual edition in the U.S. under the new title, *Generaciones y semblanzas,* trans. Rosaura Sánchez (Berkeley: Editorial Justa, 1977); *Korean Love Songs* (Berkeley: Editorial Justa, 1978); *Mi querido Rafa* (Houston: Arte Público Press, 1981); *Rites and Witnesses* (Houston: Arte Público Press, 1982); *The Valley* (Ypsilanti: Bilingual Press, 1983); and *Partners in Crime: A Rafe Buenrostro Mystery* (Houston: Arte Público Press, 1985). All citations come from the aforementioned editions.

[2]For a radical reconceptualization of the novel and its analysis, see Mikhail M. Bakhtin's *The Dialogic Imagination: Four Essays,* ed. Michael Holquist, trans. by Caryl Emerson and Michael Holquist (Austin: University of Texas Press, 1981). According to Bakhtin, the novel is a genre, in contradistinction to such fixed genres as epic and lyric, which has the ability to speak out in the most diverse and often conflicting voices. Put simply, the novel, says Bakhtin, is "dialogic," that is, an interaction of utterances, a "polyphonic" multiplicity of voices and meanings.

[3]See my interview with Rolando Hinojosa entitled "Our Southwest," published in this volume.

[4]Fredric Jameson, "Imaginary and Symbolic in Lacan: Marxism, Psychoanalytic Criticism, and the Problem of the Subject," *Yale French Studies,* 55/56 (1977) note 4, p. 340.

[5]For biographical information on Rolando Hinojosa, I have relied upon Bruce-Novoa's *Chicano Authors: Inquiry by Interview* (Austin: University of Texas Press, 1980), Rolando Hinojosa's fine article entitled "This Writer's Sense of Place" which first appeared in *The Texas Literary Tradition: Fiction, Folklore, History* (Austin: College of Liberal Arts, University of Texas, 1983), pp. 120-124, and my own formal and informal conversations with the author.

[6]Bruce-Novoa, *Chicano Authors,* p. 49.

[7]Unfortunately, closer to home in Texas, Rolando Hinojosa's work remains marginalized and ignored. For instance, not one of Hinojosa's books is to be found listed in A.C. Greene's book, *50 Best Texas Books* (1981). It is not my purpose here to catalog the ways in which the literary works of Chicanos and Chicanas have been, to a great extent, ignored, belittled or discarded in Texas and the United States. Nevertheless, it must be stressed that in control of literary tastes and publishing houses in the United States has been an all-male, all white club which has decreed that one type of experience — its own — is valuable and significant.

[8]José David Saldívar, "Our Southwest," published in this volume.

[9]For a cogent discussion of the ideology of form in literature, see Fredric Jameson's *The Political Unconscious: Narrative as a Socially Symbolic Act* (Ithaca: Cornell University Press, 1981).

[10]The phrase "the political unconscious" is, of course, Fredric Jameson's. What Jameson means by his useful phrase is the collective denial or suppression of the underlying historical contradictions in society.

[11]Rolando Hinojosa, "The Sense of Place," published in this volume.

[12]See David Montejano's *A Journey Through Mexican Texas: The Making of a Segregated Society, 1900-1930,* unpublished Ph.D. dissertation, Yale University, 1982. Montejano's extraordinary study, I believe, furnishes the socioeconomic and historical setting for all of Hinojosa's fiction whose scene is Mexican Texas.

[13]Rolando Hinojosa, "Con el pie en el estribo," *Generaciones, Notas y Brechas,* trans. Fausto Avendaño (San Francisco: Casa Editorial, 1978), p. 7.

[14]In classical Marxism, reification is the act of transforming human beings, relations, and actions into properties. See Georg Lukács' *History and Class Consciousness* (Cambridge: Massachusetts Institute of Technology Press, 1971).

[15]Bakhtin, *The Dialogic Imagination,* pp. 301-331.

[16]Hinojosa, "The Sense of Place," published in this volume.

[17]For an examination of ethnopoetics and the negative, see my essay "Towards a Chicano Poetics: The Making of the Chicano-Chicana Subject, 1968-1985," (forthcoming).

[18]My own reading of *power* in Hinojosa's *Klail City Death Trip* is indebted heavily to the work of the late Michel Foucault. From the very beginnings of his work, Foucault was concerned with the emergence, expansion, and consolidation of apparatuses of administrative intervention in, and control over, the social world. See Foucault's *The Order of Things: An Archaeology of the Human Sciences* (New York: Random House, 1970), *The Archaeology of Knowledge* (New York: Harper and Row, 1972), *Discipline and Punish: The Birth of the Prison* (New York: Pantheon Books, 1977), and *The History of Sexuality, Vol. I* (New York: Random House, 1978).

[19]Bakhtin, *The Dialogic Imagination,* p. 250.

[20]Although I cannnot provide a genuinely feminist reading of Hinojosa's *KCDT* series, I have used the works of Gayatri C. Spivak and Jane Marcus to elucidate my own critical thoughts.

[21]See Hayden White's *Metahistory: The Historical Imagination in Nineteenth-Century Europe* (Baltimore: Johns Hopkins University Press, 1973).

[22]See Tom Zigal's and Pat Jasper's "Viewpoint: A Conversation with Rolando Hinojosa-Smith," in *Texas Arts* (Summer 1983), p. 8.

[23]My reading of *Partners in Crime* is influenced by Max Horkheimer's essay entitled "The End of Reason," reprinted in *The Essential Frankfurt School Reader,* eds. Arato and Gebhardt (New York: Continuum, 1982), pp. 26-49.

[24]In his essay "Chronotope of the Novel," Bakhtin says of the historical novel, "For a long time the central and almost sole theme of the purely historical novel was the theme of war. This fundamentally historical theme — which has other motifs to it, such as conquest, political crimes, . . . dynastic revolutions, the fall of kingdoms, the founding of new kingdoms and so forth — is interwoven with personal life narrative of historical figures. . . . The major task of the modern historical novel has been to overcome this duality: attempts have been made to find an historical aspect of private life, and also to represent history in its domestic light". See Bakhtin's *The Dialogic Imagination,* p. 217. This is precisely what Hinojosa achieves in his *Klail City Death Trip* series.

Maria I. Duke dos Santos
East Texas State University

Patricia de la Fuente
Pan American University

The Elliptic Female Presence as Unifying Force in the
Novels of Rolando Hinojosa

Rolando Hinojosa has written a series of novels which comprise the "chronicles" of the mythical Belken County in the state of Texas. The main cities in this county are Flora, Klail City, Bascom, Jonesville-on-the-River and Edgerton, which the author populates with a gallery of characters sketched with brief but penetrating strokes, creating what he calls "estampas" of the people and events in this fictional replica of the Rio Grande Valley area.

The novels *Estampas del valle y otras obras* (1973) and *Generaciones y semblanzas* (1977), written in Spanish, reflect what critics have called "diferentes niveles de la expresión lingüística chicana."[1] The author reveals a deep understanding of human nature in all its facets, and in particular the intricacies of feminine psychology, although always within the context of Chicano culture, because, as he puts it, "El número de bolillos que aparece en estos escritos es bien poco."[2] In *Mi querido Rafa* (1981), also written in Spanish and in epistolary style, the author includes more English since his focus is upon a younger generation of Chicanos who can function with ease in both languages. Hinojosa justifies his use of both languages as follows: "Si se hablan ambos idiomas así saldrán también. También es natural que la raza del Valle hable mas en español. Ahora, si la raza sale en inglés, así se reportará."[3] The fourth novel, *Rites and Witnesses* (1982), written in English and in dialogue form, focuses extensively on the Angloamericans who live in the area.

Hinojosa's principal characters, together with their families, friends and enemies, appear in all four novels, giving a sense of continuity to his work. An integral part of Hinojosa's creative technique is his development of the female characters, some of whom take on an additional stylistic importance since they contribute to the structural unity and coherence of the anecdotal narrative which is one of the author's trademarks.

Among the women who most contribute to maintaining this illusion of fluidity which gives Hinojosa's style a sense of historical coherence, two stand out because of their recurring presence as ellipses whose function seems to be to intertwine the threads of different plots and characters throughout the novels. Of these elliptical characters, the most significant is Viola Barragán, "mujer bravía y de mucho ovario" (*Mi querido Rafa,* p. 27), who plays a significant role in the destiny of the mythical Belken County and in the events that alter the lives of its various inhabitants. The other is Olivia San Esteban, a pharmacist, who shares many of Viola's personal characteristics, such as a strong sense of independence and professionalism in the way they conduct their lives, often overstepping the strict boundaries of traditional or conventional feminine behavior. In both cases, Hinojosa goes beyond the development of mere character to create an elliptic female "presence" whose influence is felt as a structuring force throughout the conversations, actions and decisions of the other characters.

From the moment Viola appears in *Estampas del valle,* it is obvious that she has an atypical personality, contrasting vividly with the usual stereotype of the Hispanic woman as chaste, reserved, and dependent on a male, be he husband, father, brother, or son. An example of this stereotype is Marta Castañeda, whose sole concern appears to be the fear of being left unprotected by a male presence after her brother Balde had been jailed for killing Ernesto Támez: "Mamá y yo estamos solas pero gracias a Dios que todavía tengo a Beto. Ojalá que los Támez no vengan a buscarle bulla a él porque entonces sí que nos hundimos mamá y yo sin un hombre en casa" (*Estampas,* p. 98). This is ironic, since Beto Castañeda, Marta's husband, dies of cancer at the age of thirty-two, leaving her and her mother alone (*Estampas,* p. 130). Tradition has imposed this female image in most Hispanic countries; to stray from this idealized mode is to break with the established mores, becoming an outcast in a society that adheres to rigid standards of behavior. Viola, however, successfuly challenges these traditional values, even though her upbringing was probably as conventional as that of any of her contemporaries. Her formal education was limited since she married very young and became a widow at the age of eighteen. After a brief liaison with Javier Leguizamón, a married man twenty years her senior, however, "la viudita se despabiló" (*Estampas*, p. 119).

Viola reveals her uncommon personality through a simple but significant gesture during the funeral of her lover, Pioquinto Reyes. When everyone has gone and she is alone in the cemetery except for the young witness Rafa Buenrostro, she calmly buries a gold ring, obviously a present from her dead lover, at his graveside. "Nada de rezos ni llorisqueos sino, más bien, una mirada resignada con la frente alta, la vista despejada, y sin la menor mueca traidora en la boca" (*Estampas,* p. 119). The young narrator witnesses and records Viola's inner strength and self-reliance. The act of burying the ring could be interpreted as an expression of sincere affection; the ring, symbol of the love that united them in life, will remain with him forever in death. However, since Viola is a realist, it is entirely possible that the action also reflects her decision that the memory of her relationship with Pioquinto Reyes should be buried with him, while she continues her life in search of new friends and relationships. Indeed, at age fifty Viola is married again, and later widowed for the third time (*Mi querido Rafa,* pp. 27, 70).

Although Hinojosa uses the same technique of the elliptic character to trace the influence of these two female protagonists as a loosely knit connective for his narrative, Olivia's presence is limited to the events covered in *Mi querido Rafa,* whereas Viola's presence is felt persistently and in more detail throughout all of Hinojosa's novels. Both women possess certain characteristics that set them apart within a community notoriously reactionary in its ideas concerning women's rights and freedoms. The main difference is that Viola Barragán belongs to the previous generation, and thus her character is developed from the beginning through episodes designed to establish and strengthen her psychic bond with the reader. Within the story of her life, which the author gradually unfolds in brief sketches typical of his narrative style, Viola unexpectedly shows that, though she has a strong and aggressively mocking personality, she can also be tender and congenial. This paradox, rather than implying an inconsistency within Viola's personality, tends to humanize her and lend credibility to her as a character.

Another example of Hinojosa's use of paradox to strengthen his characterization of the unconventional Viola occurs when she takes the initiative in selecting Pioquinto Reyes as her new lover, a move which departs significantly from the behavioral norm of her social context. Viola chose him, the narrator makes perfectly clear, because she liked what she saw: "Este es de los míos; ahora hago lo que hago porque me da la gana y no por comer caliente" (*Estampas*, p. 120). This somewhat ironic honesty on the part of the narrator, and his almost defiant manner in relating this episode, rubs off on Viola and this character acquires certain subtle and realistic nuances as the narrative progresses.

Viola's comment indicates that her previous marital and extra-marital relationships were based on economic considerations rather than romantic involvement, a common occurrence among women who lack sufficient knowledge or training to face life on their own. In the case of Pioquinto Reyes, however, mutual attraction is the principal motive; and Viola's attitude deviates significantly from the traditional norm which requires an aggressive approach from the man and a passive role from the woman. The fact that Viola disregards tradition and does not hesitate to act boldly to insure her own happiness and well-being, establishes her, within the context of Hinojosa's novels, as a precursor of the contemporary Hispanic woman. In particular, Viola foreshadows Olivia San Esteban, who will act with equal maturity and determination in her relationship with Jehú Malacara, in spite of the pressure exerted upon her by the community to conform to the social convention of matrimony.

Hinojosa introduces and develops these two female characters in a similar suggestive manner through both the narrative and the dialogue. As a consequence, Viola Barragán and Olivia San Esteban gradually emerge not only as directive forces within the narrative and ultimately as significant personalities in their own right, but principally as characters who mold and influence the events around them.

One of the circumstances which contributes to establishing Viola's presence as a social and economic influence within the socio-political environment of Belken County is her knowledge of the world outside the Valley and her wealth. Her second marriage to a German diplomat not only provided her with the opportunity to live abroad for many years, but also gave her a solid financial position after his death. When she returned to the Valley, "se compró una casona; recogió a sus padres; no se olvidó en nada de sus parientes y conocidos; y, aparentemente, se retiró de su vida andariega y aventurera" (*Estampas*, p. 119). Evidently, the strong will which drives her to seek new goals in her life is tempered by a deep sense of loyalty and affection towards her family and friends. Such qualities will facilitate her role as mentor and advisor within the isolated world of Belken County.

In *Generaciones y semblanzas*, Hinojosa provides more details concerning Viola's adventures and her world travels in the company of her faithful German husband. Her experiences are extensive and varied, including a term of imprisonment in a concentration camp in India during the Second World War. During this period of her life she acquired the education she did not receive as a child; life was a good teacher and through exposure to it, Viola experienced inner growth and defined her personality. Her reality expanded beyond the confines of the Chicano experience and became universal: "Viola es una de estas personas escogidas; ella ha cruzado ríos y mares y ha enterrado a más de dos . . ." (*Mi querido Rafa*, p. 63).

In the third novel, *Mi querido Rafa*, Viola has established herself as an essential protagonist within Hinojosa's narrative. Through the narrators Jehú Malacara and P. Galindo, we know that she has become an influential presence in Belken County, appreciated by all who know her, both the Anglos (who are impressed by her influence on local business and politics) and the Chicanos (who are aware of her human qualities). Galindo compares her to "un fierro sin moho" and defines her as "amiga de sus amigos, leal y luchadora, independiente, desacobardada y firme repositorio de todo lo bueno y lo malo del Valle" (*Mi querido Rafa,* p. 63).

Her concern for her friends is evident when Jehú writes to his cousin and friend, Rafa Buenrostro, that Viola "Se acordó mucho de tí; le di tu dirección y — conociéndola — te ha de mandar regalo" (*Mi querido Rafa,* p. 27). To a far greater degree than Olivia, Viola exerts a positive influence on the community in which she lives by helping those who need it. Jehú owes her, in part, his job at Noddy Perkins' bank, since Perkins, as Jehú well knows, is one of the Anglos who listens to her advice: "A mí me ocupó por la buena recomendación de Viola B" (Mi querido Rafa, p. 26). Later on, in another letter to Rafa, Jehú again recognizes his debt to Viola: "Pero anda tú; ¿crees, in your heart of hearts, que nuestros amigos de la raza me ayudarían si necesitara chamba de repente? Aside from Viola, no lo hicieron cuando pudieron and now?" (p. 41). Viola has become a woman of high finance, a first-rate businesswoman, and has used her husband's inheritance wisely. This ability, so prized by the local Anglos, is revealed in Jehú's comments: "Viola and I talked about the bank, about my work, and — as usual — about business. She is thinking of buying some drive-in theatres and I told her 'that she's a preferred customer' (which she knows better than I)" (*Mi querido Rafa,* p. 27).

She has an open personality and enjoys a cordial relationship with her friends, with whom she jokes easily with that linguistic informality of the Chicano dialect: " 'Lo que quiero saber, flaco cabrón (Jehú), es cuándo te casas para darte un arrejuntón la semana antes' " (*Mi querido Rafa,* p. 27). Viola is a product of her cultural environment and is proud of it, without pretension or hypocrisy. She is dynamic and self-motivated: "Viola Barragán, el azote del Valle, pasó por aquí como chiflón de aire . . ." (*Mi querido Rafa,* p. 48), and even the passing of time has treated her gently, since "ahora a los cincuenta y pico de años todavía se defiende bastante bien contra el tiempo" (*Estampas,* p. 20).

In the fourth novel, *Rites and Witnesses,* the plot develops primarily around the rich, powerful Anglos of Belken County, who control the economy and politics of the region. Viola is mentioned only briefly but in a manner which confirms the position she has forged for herself in the county. Although Viola is a female in a notoriously sexist society and belongs to a minority group within the Anglo social system, she has managed to break away from both traditions and establish herself as an individual, rising above the discriminatory restrictions on women and Chicanos. Proof of this independence is the fact that Noddy Perkins, the sage, powerful banker, takes Viola's opinion into consideration, especially her recommendation of Jehú Malacara, in an episode which contrasts her altruistic attitude with the overt hypocrisy of the bankers:

> Viola recommended him, Junior.
> What's Viola's stake in all of this?
> She just wants to help him out, that's all.
> And at the same time, we do Viola a good turn.
> What for?
> Two things: future need and good business for now.[4]

Noddy realized that Viola's support would be valuable to him in the future. Later, when Noddy wants to install Ira Escobar as a political candidate, the fact that Ira's mother-in-law is a friend of Viola's influences Noddy's choice (*Rites,* p. 24).

These same techniques of developing the personality and extending the influence of Viola Barragán in all four novels is repeated in Hinojosa's third novel, *Mi querido Rafa,* when he introduces Olivia San Esteban. Olivia is the semi-official girlfriend of Jehú Malacara, one of the principal characters who moves through the novels and the author of the letters to Rafa Buenrostro, who is hospitalized in William Barrett Veteran's Hospital.

Hinojosa introduces this new elliptic female character somewhat inconspicuously in one of the many letters Jehú writes to his cousin. Olivia's importance, however, is subtly underscored in her humorous, mocking personality which immediately suggests a parallel with Viola Barragán. In describing a barbeque in honor of candidate Ira Escobar, Jehú adds:

> Invité a Olivia San Esteban (Hi there!). Yo no me pierdo de nada, tú. ¿Te acuerdas de Oli? Se hizo farmacéutica después de enseñar dos o tres años; & now she's in partnership with good old Martin el cervecero que tan mala fama cobró cuando estaba en Austin con nosotros . . .
>
> . . . la esposa de Ira . . . le dijo a Oli que ella había ido a North Texas State: a music major. Y que era miembro del Women's Club . . . le preguntó a Oli: "Do you belong Ollie?"
>
> Oli le dijo que su mamá no la dejaba salir de día y por poco se me sale la cerveza por las narices (*Mi querido Rafa,* p. 19).

This ironic reaction to the malicious and pretentious question of Rebecca Escobar clearly reveals Olivia's maturity in rejecting such social hypocrisies and mocking Becky's obvious intention to parade her membership in the Anglo Women's club. Olivia's reaction also underscores her humorous view of life and an innate self-confidence reminiscent of the anti-conventional attitudes of Viola Barragán. A significant coda to this scene is the fact that, at the conclusion of Noddy Perkins' barbeque, it is Jehú and Olivia, rather than Ira and his condescending wife, who finish the evening drinking coffee at the Klail City Diner until one in the morning with Noddy himself, Junior Klail and his wife.

This initial characterization of Olivia establishes several important details which the author will develop as the narrative progresses. In the first place, links with the past are clearly being forged here. Jehu's question: ¿Te acuerdas de Oli?" confers a certain depth and validity to a character mentioned here for the first time. By giving her a past in common with Rafa and Jehú, the author incorporates Olivia firmly into his panoramic history of Belken County. Secondly, this first scene verifies her stance as a woman free of traditional tyrannies and conventions. It also suggests a parallel with Viola in her deviation from the Hispanic female stereotypes as evidenced in Olivia's profession as a pharmacist, her college career, her brother Martin, and her mocking rejection of the social conventions represented by the status-conscious Becky Escobar.

In the third place, this initial scene between Jehú and Olivia defines her as a woman capable of confronting the political, economic, and social world of the Valley without inhibitions and of fraternizing with Noddy Perkins much as Viola is able to do. Perhaps the most startling aspect of Olivia's characterization is not so much her personal likeness to Viola Barragán, but the stylistic parallel established between them in assigning similar narrative functions to both female characters within the total structure of the novel. As already noted, the sporadic yet consistent references to the presence — explicit or implicit — of Viola Barragán help to maintain the narrative thread throughout the series of short sketches or scenes which are often anecdotal and disconnected. Hinojosa achieves a similar unifying device in the development of the character of Olivia throughout the third novel.

The action of *Mi querido Rafa* develops on several levels, the most important of which explores the relationships established by the main character, Jehú Malacara. These include economic ties, represented in his job at the Bank with Noddy Perkins; political ties, developed through Jehú's observations on county politics and the campaign of Ira Escobar; and personal ties, revealed in his intimate comments to his cousin Rafa and his growing relationship with Olivia San Esteban.

On each of these levels, Jehú is intimately involved with a woman: Sammie Jo, the frivolous daughter of Noddy Perkins, on the business level, Becky Escobar, Ira's wife on the political level, and Olivia in his personal world. The first two, however, are merely affairs in the life of a single man, and Jehú clearly evaluates them in terms of Olivia's presence: "la Sammie Jo . . . as we both know, tiene buena pierna; take my word cuando te digo que no le gana a Oli . . ." (p. 22). As for Becky, "she doesn't rank among the best . . . ¿Pero quién se queja? A one shot affair y no espero que se repita aunque you never can tell" (p. 40).

Olivia's influence in Jehú's life is far more profound and meaningful. While Sammie Jo lives a hedonistic, directionless existence, Becky naively imagines that the local Anglos have accepted her into their circle, never suspecting that in actual fact both she and Ira are puppets manipulated by Noddy Perkins. Olivia, on the other hand and according to P. Galindo, "tiene un sentido de humor así también como una idea propia de como es y de como se ve ella misma" (p. 69). Jehú himself, in his confrontation with Noddy, emphatically defends the nature of his relationship with Olivia: "Then who the hell are you talking about? And it sure as hell better not be Ollie cause that's my business . . . Goddamit" (p. 46), while openly admitting his casual liaison with Becky: "Becky and I had a couple of tussles, but that was it" (p. 46).

As the novel progresses, the name of Olivia becomes increasingly pervasive in Jehú's letters to his cousin, as does her growing influence over his life. At first the references are incidental, almost inconsequential, as in "sigo viendo a Oli de vez en cuando" (p. 21); "Olivia y yo . . . decidimos ir a Flora a cenar" (p. 33), and rather tentative, "Ollie and I are going to Barrones, Tamps. for a night-weekend on the town. More (or less) on this at a later time" (p. 29). Later, a certain familiarity creeps into the relationship: "Este fin de semana, Olivia y yo, como sabes, andábamos para arriba y para abajo" (p. 38), until gradually the presence of Olivia begins to determine the direction of Jehú's life: "I needed to be with Oli more than just overnight" (p. 50).

But in spite of local speculation and gossip, and the approval of Viola Barragán, who teases her protegé good-naturedly ("ah, y que no se te olvide de mandarme invitación al casorio, oíste?") (p. 48), neither Jehú nor Olivia fit the conventional mold of an engaged couple. In her interview with P. Galindo, Olivia expresses her self-confidence, claiming that "una no es como se crió sino como se es y yo soy así" (p. 69), and clarifying the untraditional but satisfying relationship she shares with Jehú: "Cuando vuelva de donde ande, volverá por mí. Y si no para casarnos, no importa; él y yo nos entendemos" (p. 69).

The evidence suggests that in Olivia San Esteban, the author not only created a small-scale replica of his most attractive and outstanding female character, Viola Barragán, but that he also gave her the same "elliptic" characteristics enjoyed by Viola in the four novels. Not only is Viola one of the most outstanding and functional characters within the structure of Hinojosa's sketches, but she is also the most fully developed and well-rounded of all the female characters in his novels. Besides being a linking force connecting many of the characters and incidents in these novels, Viola plays a significant role in the general perspective of Belken County because she affects many of its inhabitants with her forceful personality, her wealth, and her good-natured desire to help others.

In both cases, the author seems to have been seduced by his own creations. Among other things, he has bestowed on Viola and Olivia physical beauty, common sense, intelligence, attractive personalities, good naturedness, and — especially in the case of Viola Barragán — an abundance of wealth. No other character in the novels speaks unkindly of them. The image that they both project is that of self-confident women who know where they are coming from and who use their accumulated experience to focus clearly on the future. Both women know where they are going and recognize their personal goals. Both have overcome traditional sexist restrictions to enter a challenging, once forbidden world.

One could say, therefore, that in creating independent, dynamic female characters such as Viola Barragán and Olivia San Esteban, and by using them — particularly in the case of Viola — as elliptic characters with explicit catalytic functions within the narrative, Hinojosa achieves maximum unity and cohesion in a novelistic style which is inherently anecdotal and loosely knit. It is not a coincidence that these two characters represent what could be called the image of the new Hispanic woman in the Americas. In creating them, Hinojosa issues an unequivocal affirmation of the potential of the contemporary Hispanic woman in the urban environment, concentrating the unity of his narrative style in these characters whose complexity reflects the unstable and contradictory sensibility of our modern age.[5]

[1]Herminio Ríos C., "Introduction," in Rolando R. Hinojosa's *Estampas del valle y otras obras* (Berkeley: Quinto Sol Publications, 1973), p. 8.

[2]Rolando R. Hinojosa, *Generaciones y semblanzas* (Berkeley,: Editorial Justa Publications, 1977), p. 1.

[3]Rolando Hinojosa, *Mi querido Rafa* (Houston: Arte Público Press, 1981), p. 8.

[4]Rolando Hinojosa, *Rites and Witnesses* (Houston: Arte Público Press, 1982), pp. 7 and 9.

[5]This essay was presented in a condensed version at the XXIII Congreso del Instituto Internacional de Literatura Iberoamericana, in Madrid, Spain, June 25-29, 1984.

Rosaura Sánchez
University of California, San Diego

From Heterogeneity to Contradiction: Hinojosa's Novel

The five books[1] by Rolando Hinojosa constitute a macrotext — one novel chronicling the lives of several generations of Chicanos in the Valley of Texas. As a unitary text with a macrostructure within which are articulated the microstructures (that is, the individual volumes), the novel is dynamic and reflects the various transformations in the history of the community. As individual works, on the other hand, the texts appear to be fragmented, static, and monocentric, developing on one plane only with a heterogeneity of characters and events. Since there is one more text to appear (*Claros varones de Belken County*), one could even say the novel is a work still in process.

The novel at this point is divided into five books. Two reflect the heterogeneity of everyday life in the Chicano/Mexicano community of the fictional "Belken County" in South Texas, and two focus on the private and business affairs of the ruling-class Anglo family in Klail City. The fifth, a transitional collection of narrative poems recounting events in Korea, serves to connect the whole and to mark two distinct periods of time: before and after the Korean War. The novel itself consists of a series of sketches, interviews, testimonials, monologues and dialogues arranged in the first two books within a spiral structure which allows the narrators to circle continuously around the same center and on one plane, even as the curves increase and decrease as more or less information is provided about new or previously seen events and characters. But while the first two books are limited to a view of heterogeneity in the community, the last two books explore the social and class contradictions in the Valley. It is the fragmentation and brief "capsule" style of each account reducing different phases and periods of time to one plane which decontextualize events so that the impact of history or social change on individual lives and on particular social classes is not evident. The incorporation of other planes and dimensions in the fourth and fifth books serves to round out the novel and provides a necessary dimension and depth.

The author's intent in his compilation of sketches of everyday life in the Chicano community is clear in introductory remarks to various sections:

> Aquí no hay héroes de leyenda: esta gente va al escusado, estornuda, se limpia los mocos, cría familias, conoce lo que es morir con el ojo pelón, se cuartea con dificultad y (como madera verde) resiste rajarse. El que busque héroes de la proporción del Cid, pongamos por caso, que se vaya a la laguna de la leche.[2]

This "cronicón del condado de Belken y su gente"[3] is exactly that, a chronicle of segments of Belken County life. The books are narrated from the perspective of the decade of the '70s as the narrators look back to the '30s, '40s and '50s and even beyond, to the early part of the 20th century. In these various periods the community faced threats from the outside, from the Anglo world; but apparently it remained largely segregated, a world unto itself, generation after generation. The Mexican Valley remained an idyllic place where the collective spirit reigned amidst heterogeneity.

These static sketches, however, are fraught with underlying contradictions; here and there one catches rapid anecdotal references to cases of oppression and resistance. But it is only in the last two books that the destruction of the Valley idyll is complete and that social contradictions beyond ethnicity become manifest.

The novel's movement from heterogeneity to contradiction will be analyzed in terms of the text's time-space framework and its intertextuality, with a focus on the novel's dialogue with history.

Intertextuality and heteroglossia

The novel, states Bakhtin, is "a phenomenon multiform in style and variform in speech and voice."[4] A diversity of social speech varieties or languages and individual voices are artistically combined and orchestrated in a given way to produce a particular novelistic style. Bakhtin's analysis of heteroglossia and intertextuality can be useful in an analysis of Hinojosa's novel which is characterized by this very mutliplicity of voices.

There is within the Hinojosa novel an intersection of various styles, modes and language varieties as well as code-shifting in the discourse of characters and narrators. The novel dialogues as well with various forms of literary and semiliterary styles, with folklore, popular culture and foremost with history. It is this intertextuality and the particular heterogeneous combination of language and styles that we will first describe, before focusing on the individual works.

The novel's literary intertextuality is evident in the variety of stylistic forms and literary techniques which continually intersect in the novel. Even in its titles, the books dialogue with literary history. *Estampas* could be a reference to the sketches of manners published since the 18th century in European newsletters and newspapers. These sketches or "cuadros de costumbres" were characterized by their brevity and by their portrayals of individuals, cities and towns, often serving as travel guides, and assuming various forms: sketches, letters, diaries, dialogues and monologues. These short, anecdotal pieces were often humorous and sometimes satirical; although generally portrayals of local color, some were psychological studies of individuals from the ruling classes.

This type of writing, however, can be traced back even further to historical chronicles of 15th and 16th-century Spanish kingdoms. The "cronicón del valle" similarly records the founding of the Texas Valley and the births and deaths in the principal extended family — la familia Buenrostro — through several generations, with references to settlements dating back to the 19th century. The best known "estampas" or "cuadros" in Spanish literature are sketches by 19th century Spanish *costumbristas,* like Serafín Estébanez Calderón, Ramón de Mesonero Romanos and Mariano José de Larra. Here, however, one would have to distinguish between two types of sketches, those like Larra's, satirical in nature which describe class contradictions in society, and those portraying individuals, traditions and social practices while revealing a certain nostalgia for the past.[5]

Although Hinojosa's sketches are not satirical, his first two books do look back with irony and nostalgia on earlier periods to reveal a rural society in transition. The everyday lives of towns-people in Klail City, however, are not revealed in all domains. The novel, for example, does not enter the work site. What predominates throughout the novel is the area of interpersonal relations, whether it be on the road, in the cantina, at the cardgame room or at the park. This informal domain when situated in the home or office of the wealthy Anglos will contrast markedly with scenes from the Korean battlefield. The other domain is that of the "past," whether remote or recent, brought into play through letters and dialogues, and segments of reverie recalling particular individuals or humorous/tragic episodes.

By the decade of the '70s, the transition is complete as entrepreneurial interests come to dominate the Valley economy. The effects of these transformations on the largely agricultural work force, however, are not the focus here. The novel has no sketches of the destitute, the unemployed, the illiterate, or the poverty-stricken, despite the Valley's high poverty rate. There are no alienated, exhausted or frustrated men and women here as in the work of Tomás Rivera. Nevertheless, the characters are many and diverse: professionals, public officials, farmers, ranch hands, businessmen, shopkeepers, candy vendors, sweepers, truckdrivers, electricians, bartenders and the retired, all seen outside the work place in an informal camaraderie where social stratification, except that arising from age differences, is indistinct. For a moment we hear briefly of migration and of accidents of migrants on the long road to the Midwest. But these references are anecdotal and merely serve to round out the collective portrayal which is the focus of the novel.

The title of the second book is easily traceable to the 15th century *Generaciones y semblanzas,* written around 1450 by

Fernán Pérez de Guzmán. The text, a collection of sketches of famous personages of the reign of Henry III (1390-1406) and John II (1406-54), provided physical, social, and moral characteristics of the ruling class.[6] The genre was continued in the same century by Hernando del Pulgar, author of *Claros varones de Castilla,* the source of Hinojosa's unpublished title, *Claros varones de Belken County.* Unlike the Pérez de Guzmán sketches, the Pulgar portraits were characterized by their irony and humor, although again they focused on ruling class characters.[7] As we shall see, irony and humor are the outstanding characteristics of the Hinojosa novel.

Of special interest to an analysis of Hinojosa's work is the picaresque and particularly *El Lazarillo de Tormes,* which integrates the satirical and the folkloric by placing the rogue on the road through familiar 16th century Spanish territory to expose and criticize a series of social conventions and moral values. Its concise narrative style as well as the hero's adaptation to the corruption he first did not understand[8] are helpful in understanding the sketches of Jehú in the Hinojosa novel.

Equally important as literary antecedents are numerous works by Latin American writers like Ricardo Palma, Tomás Carrasquilla, Roberto Payró, José Rubén Romero, Alberto Gerchunoff and many others. The sketches provided in their works include historical anecdotes and picturesque descriptions in a humorous vein of regions and provincial life. Like many of these sketches, Hinojosa's are based on a comic incident, providing insight into the attitudes and idiosyncrasies of ordinary people through their own dialogues and monologues, thereby producing an air of familiarity.

Hinojosa's novel is thus rich in intertextuality as texts of diverse origin intersect the novel creating varied and multigeneric stylistic patterns. The most obvious, as we have seen, are the literary texts with which the novel dialogues.

The author's narration is in fact a constant response to literary history. Goffman, like Bakhtin, has stated that discourse is always a response.[9] Moreover, Bakhtin adds, it always necessarily incorporates or appropriates previous discourse, one's own and that of others.[10] Hinojosa's work thus revitalizes several generations of Spanish and Latin American literary history through his adaptation and incorporation of generic forms that date back to the 15th century. But his work also dialogues extensively with Chicano/Mexicano history and even with figures of present history, as is the case of his ongoing dialogue with José Limón, Américo Paredes and Octavio Romano in the texts.

The history continually intersecting the Hinojosa novel is the history of the population of Mexican origin in the Texas Valley. The novel captures the racial, national and linguistic fragmentation of the Valley, as well as its bilingualism and the inter-ethnic alliances established within the propertied classes. Economic and social relations between classes are not always clear, however. In the first two books, the Anglo population appears as peripheral, marginal to the issue, as the narrator himself indicates in the introduction to *Generaciones y semblanzas*:

> El número de bolillos que se ve en estos escritos es bien poco. Los bolillos están, como quien dice, al margen de estos sucesos. A la raza de Belken, la gringada le viene ancha; por su parte, la gringada, claro es, como está en poder, hace caso a la raza cuando le conviene: elecciones, guerra, susto económico, etc. (Las cosas más vale decirse como son si no, no.)[11]

The Anglos' peripheral status, however, is only an illusion, for they control, for the most part, the economic life of the entire Valley as well as the political structure, as the last two books make clear. However, antagonism between Anglos and Mexicanos is not absent from the text of the first two books, given a smattering of references to cases like those of Ambrosio Mora (a W.W.II veteran killed by a sheriff's deputy cleared of all charges in the murder) and to the alliance of white land developers with the Texas Rangers to gain possession of land owned by Mexicanos.

Clashes between the two populations over land in the early part of the 20th century serve as a continual backdrop to the sketches, as evidenced in the Buenrostro episodes or in relation to don Manuel Guzmán's land loss while serving in Obregón's army during the Mexican Revolution, despite the fact that their mention is rapid and anecdotal. Thus history continually intersects the novel almost as a fleeing specter. These references would require additional information for decoding what De León describes as a situation of harrassment, persecution and depredations of Tejanos.[12] Yet, sketches in the first two books do not reveal the fate of the thousands of homeless families who lost their land and had to rent or sell their labor time as farmworkers.[13] The one example in the novel, don Manuel, continued to do well after being robbed of his land. Migrant labor, moreover, is not directly linked to land loss in the novel.

The landgrabbing, intermarrying and alliances of families nevertheless form a historical backdrop to the narration as this historical thread appears and reappears, intersecting various sketches. Of course life in Texas during the last part of the 19th century and early 20th century went beyond competition for land. Mexicans were murdered in cold blood by Anglos suspecting them of cattle rustling[14] or merely for being Mexican. Racial friction as well as economic rivalry continued despite economic changes which brought a shift from subsistence agriculture to commercial farming in south Texas.[15] These animosities and antagonisms are faint associations made from a distance by the older members of the community. But within the Chicano/ Mexicano community of the '30s and '40s life goes on rather idyllically, as if it were far from victimization, racism and economic and political oppression. It is only the memories of the older members of the community that serve to remind the reader of an absence that is not satisfied until the last two books.

If actual labor conditions are missing from these sketches, the complicity of Mexicanos in landgrabbing and murders is well documented, as are instances of Anglo paternalism. The narrator Galindo, for example, takes time to point out the individual efforts of one Tom Purdy, who singlehandedly fixed the living quarters provided to several migrant families.[16] The "good Anglo" sketch thus takes precedence over the brutal exploitation faced by these rural laborers in the Midwest, a situation that has been well documented by Cardenas[17] and Rubalcava[18] and described in part by Tomás Rivera.[19]

The economic and political subordination of Chicanos, however, becomes clear in the last two books. Although there is no discussion of low wages, poor working conditions, or work relations here either, there is a presentation of the economic control of the city by three Anglo families linked through marriage and blood ties. Intimate sketches of business and family life critically portray their political control of all elections in the County through subterfuge, coercion and economic manipulation, and their intricate manipulation of the legal system to gain access to land, business enterprises and millions of dollars without being subject to taxation by the government.

The novelist's dialogue with Chicano/Mexicano history goes beyond the incorporation of history to include folkloric elements (like the trickster tale which we see in his portrayal of Burnias, fooled by a farmer into accepting a worm-infested pig instead of wages, but able to turn the trick on him in the end)[20] and other popular cultural forms. The heterogeneity of the discourse is evident in the incorporation of popular sayings (particularly in the discourse of Echevarría), the Corrido form (in a discussion of the shooting of Ambrosio Mora),[21] and the "vacilada/choteo," male jive (particularly in the cantina scenes). But the novelist goes beyond these popular forms to incorporate genres from other disciplines. To the literary diary, letter, sketch and dialogue forms, Hinojosa adds segments of Radio Talk in a presentation of the Mexican D. J. Enedino Broca Lopez.[22] Moreover, he incorporates the sociological instrument of interviews (which form part of the *Mi querido Rafa* text and are extended to *Rites and Witnesses*), whereby the character Galindo researches Jehú's whereabouts, thus presenting a broad perspective of the attitudes of both Chicanos and Anglos in Klail

City. He also includes a legal deposition in the episode on Balde Cordero.[23] By incorporating all these sub-genres within the novel, Hinojosa succeeds in amalgamating discourse from every sphere of everyday life to provide a heterogeneous and multilevel view of life in the Valley.

The novel's varied collective gives rise to a multiplicity of voices — what Bakhtin calls heteroglossia.[24] Language varieties are primarily male styles of informal Spanish within an ironic and humorous mode. The cyclic repetition of the novel allows events, episodes and characterizations to be introduced by one of the male narrators (Galindo, Rafa or Jehú) or by the characters themselves in their own voices and to be later reviewed by additional characters who dialogue in the novel or are part of the interview series.

Shifts also occur within the narrators' discourse. The narrators are sometimes serious, sometimes cynical but generally good-humored as they describe the individual flaws and strengths of a multitude of characters. In a novel where loyalty to friends and blood ties are important, it is the male informal style that cements relations. This style is characterized by a racy repartee, both clever and impudent:

> Don Orfalindo Buitureyra es cabrón de nacimiento. También es farmacéutico pero eso ya es culpa del estado de Texas.

. . . .

> No. Don Orfalindo no es una mala persona. Además, eso de ser cabrón no es acto propio o sui generis o lo que sea. Don Orfalindo era don Orfalindo y entonces vino su mujer y fue ella la que lo hizo cabrón: Made in Texas by Texans, aunque, en este caso, by chicanos.
> –¿Y la prole?
> –No, la prole es de él.
> –¡Cómo no! Si todos se le parecen en la nariz . . .
> –¡Y en las quijadas! Si hasta parece que los cagó . . .

> –Conque se parecen, ¿eh?
> –Como un mojón a otro.
> –Pero es cabrón . . .
> –Bueno esa mancha no se le quita ni con gaso-
> lina . . .[25]

The ironic thus becomes burlesque as male adults elaborate the local *chismografía* at the cantina, taunting each other and casting indirect darts of sarcasm in the direction of fellow bar clients. Sexual liaisons, unfaithful wives, gambling, violent encounters and the past are some of their favorite topics of conversation. Their voices also ring out at the park to ridicule Big Foot Parkinson, a candidate for sheriff. Echevarría is equally burlesque in his scornful comments about the Texas Ranger Choche Markham, who tried to pass himself off as a friend of the Chicanos but who in fact was the lackey of the ruling class:

> Bien haya que había gente como don Julián Buenrostro que le dijo al pinche rinche que se fuera a la chingada — que él, Julián Buenrostro, cruzaba el río y se echaba al monte tras el que fuera. Y lo hizo, raza. Lo cumplió. Bien haya el que tiene los pantalones puestos y no se agacha a mear. Amigo de la raza . . . ¡Mamalón eso es lo que es Choche Markhamí En su vida ha ayudado a la raza. En su vida . . .[26]

The characters at times shift not only style and mode but language as well. Between the two younger narrators, code-switching serves not only as a sign of close friendship between cousins but also triggers a shift in mode to convey the character Jehú's need to make light of his problematic situation at the Bank, to distance himself from all the muck he describes in his letters and to play down his new importance as loan officer. English is of course the language of the ruling-class dialogues, however hispanicized these Anglos may be. Thus code-shifting in Jehú also signals assimilation.

The female voice is notable for its absence from these sketches. One would have to assume that the Valley is primarily a male world, with women as bed partners and not much else. Here and there the author introduces an exception, like the short monologue by Jehú's mother or Marta's declaration about her brother Balde, both in *Estampas*. Here and there we find an extended sketch of Viola Barragán, the enterprising widow whose life and assets are totally unrepresentative of women in the Valley. But for the most part the novel does not consider women as an important part of Valley history.

The multiplicity of characters in the novel and the continual shifts in space and voice in the first two volumes eliminate movement in time but guarantee heterogeneity and heteroglossia. The last two volumes on the other hand will introduce time and contradiction while not eliminating heteroglossia.

Estampas del valle y otras obras

Social heterogeneity is especially marked in the first book *Estampas del valle y otras obras,* which consists of an album of character sketches, episodes, and several brief annotations of anecdotes recalled by one of the novel's characters. Its heterogeneity is evident in the plurality of characters, linked by a commonality of national origin, locale, world view, language and traditions. Yet despite this multiplicity of characters, class distinctions are not evident in the sketches since the mass is presented as a heterogeneous collective within which develop conflicts and animosities between individuals, rather than between social classes. As previously indicated, the theme of loss of land by Chicanos and land appropriation and manipulation by both Anglo and Chicano landowners runs through the first volume, but the loss motif is more often developed in terms of loss of loved ones and loss of limb. The loss motif is what binds all volumes as part of the "Death Trip series."

Characters in this volume are shifted from one event to another without producing any significant shifts in time or space. In fact, the novel's fragmented and disjointed time-space produces stasis, since shifts from one character to another, from one episode to another, from one comical situation to another do not produce real movement. There is no development of plot. Despite the thread of historical events mentioned throughout the book, historical time is missing; thus recalled events function as isolated instances taken out of the temporal process. Events lead √ to no change in the lives of the characters, beyond the natural phenomena of living and dying. Wars, revolutions, sedition, crime, land loss, daily events are all seen as a chain of events on the same plane, blurring all temporal boundaries. Moreover, each character, although briefly mentioned in several sketches at different points in time, is always the same, static and immutable. Even the review of genealogical trees linking one generation to previous generations does not produce movement; here all time is fused. And despite mention of other geographical points in Mexico, the U.S., Korea, or Japan, spatial elements do not exist as an integrated part of a broader context but as disconnected points, additional settings within which the characters are said to have proved their mettle. What matters is this little spatial world with its familiar spots, where several generations of Mexicanos/Chicanos have lived and died, where an idyllic world is about to be destroyed, a world the two main characters will leave.

It is the characters' desire for change that will signal contradictions underlying the static portrayal of small-town life. Death destroys the idyllic-type family in the sketches but so do other social, economic and political events only mentioned in passing in this first book and presented in detail in the last two books (*Mi querido Rafa* and *Rites and Witnesses*). *Estampas* functions more like an author's "Notebook of themes and characters to be developed in subsequent works." Relationships are delineated and traces of social conflict, particularly in comments referring to don Javier Leguizamón, already point to what will later be further contextualized. What is merely an accumulation of events here hints at phases to come; rapid references to changes in the lives of characters suggest links to social and political changes. In subsequent volumes the fragmented sketches and notations will acquire fuller form, although many of the techniques (interviews, dialogues, sketches) will continue to be used. Eventually the structural fragmentation begins to point to social fragmentation and contradiction.

The fact that no particular character is the center of attention in this first book allows for a portrayal of social and spatial heterogeneity, but in the books that follow *Estampas* the characters Jehú and Rafa clearly become the main characters. This first work also outlines the narrative techniques to be used in subsequent volumes: throughout the novel characters will be revealed through the words of others and their own dialogue; this discourse is never self-conscious interior monologue.

Generaciones y semblanzas

Like *Estampas, Generaciones y semblanzas* would appear to have a one-plane spiral structure with the various sketches and episodes circling continuously around the same center and on one plane. Here the curves both constantly increase and decrease in size as the chronicle repeatedly reviews previously mentioned events and characters, whether in *Estampas* or in this volume, adding additional information or linking previously disconnected elements. Again the sketchy narration condensing major events and large periods of time to a few sentences reduces novelistic time to a chain of moments — instances, hours, days — on the same plane.

Throughout the first two books, distinct episodes unite various fragments of life in the Valley. The principal thread here is the Buenrostro-Leguizamón conflict which determines rivalries and loyalties in the novel. Through a few sketches, including Echevarría's monologues and other dialogues scattered throughout the texts, we learn briefly and rapidly that since earlier times the Leguizamóns were landowners allied to Anglo landowners and the Texas Rangers and interested in acquiring by hook or crook additional Belken County land, including the ranch of El Carmen, owned by the Buenrostros who had legal proof of ownership. The Leguizamóns tried to force them out, but the Buenrostros stayed put. One night someone sneaked up to the ranch and murdered don Jesús, Rafa's father, as he slept in a tent. His brother Julián, who arrived too late to save his brother, later learns who paid the killers, hunts them down and kills them. As for the Leguizamón who had hired the killers, he's soon found dead with his brains bashed in while having a rendezvous in front of the Catholic Church.

The Chicano-Anglo alliance among particular propertied families is alluded to already in *Estampas* where we learn that don Javier Leguizamón's sister was married to one of the rich Blanchards; but even before the marriage the Leguizamóns are said to have been the Anglos' lackeys and allies. Through their contacts, the Leguizamóns were able to acquire a great deal of land and later go into business establishing several clothing and food stores. The narrator's feelings toward the Leguizamóns are clear: "Javier no es chicano tampoco, es Leguizamón, y los Leguizamón, bien es sabido, no tuvieron madre; fueron hijos de tía."[27] The Buenrostros, on the other hand, are presented as the defenders of the land and protectors of others with whom they share the land. At this stage charcterization is not complex.

Events in this volume and in the entire novel affect three generations of Chicanos/Mexicanos, although there are references to former generations as well. The three include, first, those born in the last decades of the 19th century, men who left Texas to participate in the Mexican Revolution of 1910; a second generation of adults from the 1930's is only sparingly portrayed; the third generation which includes the young men during the decade of the '50s who fought in the Korean War is the most important in the novel.

By the time of the third generation, most of the land in the Valley is in the hands of the "bolillos," except in the case of those who allied themselves with the Anglos, families like the Leguizamóns, or in the case of those who resisted. Among the Chicano landowners who united against the Rangers to resist the takeover of their land were the Buenrostros.

This land conflict, however, is only one of many problems and themes spotlighted briefly in the text. Emphasis on the heterogeneous experience again precludes links to a larger context. Connections between the Chicano and Anglo Valley are almost nonexistent in this volume, except for the last three pages, where class and ethnic stratification in high school is rapidly sketched through a list of names of primarily Anglo students never before mentioned, as if the author were suddenly aware of the enormous gap. The Anglo community is thus peripheral to the first two books; only a few brief references to the "bolillos" are made, often humorous asides except in the case of the death of Ambrosio Mora.

These sketches thus present an amalgam of events, a set of social conditions, a series of character types and the language, belief system, traditions and culture of this spatial corner of the world. It is the collective plane that occupies the major part of the novel with only brief glimpses of the private lives of a multitude of characters, glimpses provided by the various narrators who function as eavesdroppers. Characters are thus viewed in isolated moments and consequently in stasis rather than in the process of becoming. Boundaries between individual lives and between various phases of one and the same life are blurred. But the fact that this world is presented in a fragmented fashion is tied to the Valley's fragmentation and threatened destruction. The decay of the Valley idyll, of idyllic type families and patriarchal relationships, is present from the beginning, but its destruction will become evident only in the last two books as the two main characters leave the Valley.

Jehú and Rafa, along with Galindo, are the principal narrators of the novel and its key protagonists, weaving through various fragments and serving to connect the various sketches. From the first the two are presented as "men of the people." They hold the "correct" attitudes toward life, death, and women. Of the two, Jehú is the most interesting. Although the intent may have been to present Jehú and Rafa as two sides of a coin (Malacara vs. Buenrostro), the double of each other, their voices are often not distinct. What makes Jehú stand out is not only his social contact as an orphan with a heterogeneous set of individuals who befriend him, but especially his weaknesses, his cockiness and his ability to change.

The character Rafa, on the other hand, is presented as a repetition of his father Jesús, the "quiet one." Like his father, Rafa is quiet, serious, noble and courageous, ever ready to lend a helping hand, whether to the mud-stained drunken Echevarría or to the wounded in Korea. He is the epitome of loyalty, as evidenced in his corroboration of Sonny Ruiz' disappearance in Korea, and he is discrete in his love affairs. Like Jehú, he too partakes of the "loss" motif, in this case the loss of loved ones through death or separation. Like several other characters, Rafa functions as an observer, an eavesdropper, who can provide eyewitness accounts of the collective experience through his musings about Klail City and his relationships with friends. References to the various periods of his life (childhood, work experience, junior high, high school, Korea, university studies) are vague and offer a fragmentary framework at best, since none of these phases is elaborated. The character moves through space, from the bar in Klail City to Korea, but his identity remains invariable, absolutely unchanged.

Jehú's ability to change does not become evident until the last two books. In the first two volumes he too appears to be congealed in the good-natured rogue role, whether he works for the circus, the bar, the missionary, or the ranch. Our first contact with Jehú is through a monologue in *Estampas* at age 34 as he recalls the past: the death of his parents, his relatives, his joining a small circus of acrobats, his relations to don Victor Peláez, a surrogate father figure, and his loss again after Don Victor's death. Throughout the first two books, Jehú also functions as narrator of the more humorous or comical aspects of everyday life in Belken County.

After the introductory circus scenes, Jehú becomes a full-fledged rogue. Like a picaresque hero, Jehú takes the road which leads him from Relámpago to Edgerton to Flora to Klail

City, all towns in Belken County. In Flora survival means serving a priest as acolyte. But after an accident resulting from his going swimming instead of covering a hole dug by two treasure hunters, Jehú decides to leave town. He then joins an itinerant protestant missionary who sells Bibles. Tomás Imás, the anglicized Chicano, allows Jehú to develop further his circus "barker" talents as he tries to sell "the Word" much like one would sell a tonic or cure-all.

The road stops in Klail City where through various sketches we briefly see the young Jehú as store sweeper, barber shop sweeper and cardgame dealer before leaving town to be a goatherder on Don Celso's ranch. Only bits and fragments of his life are reported. Later on he is said to have been adopted by the policeman, don Manuel, received an inheritance from don Victor and attended high school. The orphan to rogue to student period moves quickly. In our next contact with the character, he has become a banker after being in the army, attending the University of Texas and working as a high school teacher, but all the reader has are anecdotal references.

Mi querido Rafa

The book *Mi querido Rafa* is divided into two parts: the letters written by Jehú to his cousin Rafa Buenrostro and compiled by the narrator P. Galindo and a second part which consists of a series of interviews conducted by Galindo in Klail City to determine what actually happened to Jehú at the KBC Bank. The use of Jehú's letters allows the author to provide a personal eyewitness account of the private and business affairs of the ruling class family in Klail City while at the same time allowing us to see Jehú as a participant in the events. Although letters as a literary technique have traditionally been used to reveal a character's intimate thoughts, Jehú's letters, without being impersonal nor obscure, are rather discrete about his innermost thoughts as well as about his intimate and personal affairs. His sexual encounters, while only implicit in the letters, are the topic of several interviews. Jehú thus functions as both participant and observer, as an internal cog in the machine and as the observer of the life of others, in this case the life of the Klails, Blanchards and Cookes; and while he does meddle in their world now and then, as the chief loan officer of the Bank and as the daughter's bed partner, he does not truly belong or participate in the gringo world, much like the pícaro on the road through familiar territory who observes the personal and private life of others but is not determined by it.

Galindo's interviews, on the other hand, allow us to review the same information presented by Jehú with further elaboration by other eyewitnesses and observers. Galindo becomes a detective of sorts who attempts to piece together, with the help of various individuals' comments, the events that took Jehú from the Bank. Through these interviews we also come to see that the Ranch hands and service workers function as eavesdroppers as well, providing private and personal information about a world to which Chicanos have no access. These informants thus serve to confirm or contradict previously implied or stated information, adding a necessary complexity to the narration while exposing and portraying various layers and levels of private life.

Thus although it has retained a fragmented structure composed of brief segments, *Mi querido Rafa* provides several previously missing ingredients. The most important is historicity. Up to now all events have appeared on a vertical axis, a paradigm of characters, events, episodes within one space: Belken County. But the syntagmatic dimension placing these events in a horizontal time axis to reflect change in both history and in the characters themselves has been missing. Brief mention of historical dates formerly served only as a backdrop to events but did not project social change given the absence of in-depth characterization of individuals and the lack of interconnection between characters and their social condition.

This volume also introduces a new element: the political and economic structure of the Valley. The KBC family is now revealed as the power controlling the economic and political life of Belken County. Their bank's approval of loans determines who survives in business; their economic leverage determines elections and political appointments; with their connections and clout, they can apply pressure on any dissident sector or individual in the county, bringing that individual to his knees.

Mi querido Rafa elaborates on the land grabbing deals which left many Chicano families without land, but it goes even further. The pie is much bigger. We are no longer simply talking about land and agribusiness. The Bank represents finance capital, investments, corporations and corrupt practices. The law of the land favors them and allows them to manipulate nonprofit corporations for legal tax evasion. The political maneuvering goes beyond local politics. KBC controls all county positions as well as state and congressional seats from the area. Locally the KBC family has its Mexican/Chicano intermediary: don Javier Leguizamón, who is kept in tow with the hiring of a nephew, Ira Escobar, later the Bank's puppet in public office.

The function of Jehú, now a pseudo-rogue, and the other eavesdroppers is to expose what is false and exploitive in human relations. Like the traditional pícaro-rogue he is "level-headed, cheery, a clever wit."[28] Although not a "tramp belonging to no class",[29] as the traditional picaro, the bachelor Jehú, is not tied to KBC nor even to Klail City itself. He has, then, the necessary social distance and the chutzpah to join, then leave, the KBC organization, exposing in the process the corrupt practices of the ruling class. But as in picaresque, the exposure comes through his affiliation with the object of scorn, the Valley's ruling class, a position that allows him to comment on the family's public and personal life. His attitude wavers between surprise and then admiration of the devious and intricate handling of the law through sales, may have been to present Jehú and Rafa as two sides of a coin property without paying taxes. The political maneuvering by the Bank machine involves Jehú as chief loan officer indirectly; apparently the Bank seeks to involve him further to ensure his silence, but Jehú is neither interested in going to Washington to work in the puppet congressman's office nor in co-signing for the man's loans.

At the personal level, Jehú, like all pícaros, deceives his employers and runs the risk of being eliminated from the Bank staff or worse. This modern pícaro is not so much interested in stealing food, like el Lazarillo, but in bedding Becky Escobar, the wife of Leguizamón's nephew (KBC's latest political puppet) and Sammie Jo, the daughter of Noddy Perkins, unofficial head of the Bank. At the same time, Jehú's presence at the Bank enables him not only to observe and comment on relations between various husbands and wives but to describe the ruling family's deterioration. Politically powerful and corrupt, it is also physically and morally weak, with alcoholics, like Perkin's wife; sexual deviants, like the drunkard Sanford who forces himself on young ranch servant girls and then forces them to abort; and marriages of convenience, like that of Sammie Jo and her homosexual husband Sydney Boynton. At another level, there is a good deal of competition between the various family heads who resent the power of Noddy Perkins, who married wealthy Blanche Cooke.

As in the picaresque, the pícaro Jehú escapes, leaving everyone speculating as to his whereabouts and the reason for his unexpected departure. He is suspected by some Chicanos of having absconded with Bank funds while others suspect that his sexual encounters may have gotten him into trouble. From Jehú's letter we know that Perkins tries to fire him publicly; sensing that he is being cornered on mere suspicion and not really knowing the extent of Perkin's power game, Jehú calls his bluff and admits to have sex with Becky Escobar, while denying involvement with Sammie Jo. And he stays on at the Bank for a few more days before leaving on his own. Whether Jehú leaves for political reasons as well or simply because of his liaisons with Becky and Sammie Jo is not clear. The author prefers ambiguity at this point, but there are indications in the letters that would lead one to suspect that Jehú has gone beyond simply being a promiscuous rascal.

Jehú's brief letters to Rafa are witty, sometimes cynical, summaries of the day's events. Although at first he adjusts well to the Bank routine as the socially-mobile Chicano, he eventually finds the ruling class world disgusting: "One last thing: I don't think I'm going to last here much longer; I don't have the stomach for it."[30] And in one of his last letters to Rafa: "There must be something other than el camino lento y sosegado al camposanto de Nuestra Señora de la Merced. There must be."[31] From simply reacting, outwitting and surviving, Jehú apparently turns to self-reflection and analysis, although the process is never revealed in the text. What is implicit in some of his cryptic comments is that at some point he questions his participation in the Bank's manipulation of the economic and political affairs of the city, although on the surface Jehú appears to be simply an individual looking after his own hide. For the first time in the novel a character faces his own contradictions. Commitment to something no longer definable, no longer the idyllic community, perhaps to himself, perhaps to a few friends and a woman, pulls him in a different direction.

The character is thus no longer static nor marginal; he, too, is smeared and tainted. However, he does not propose to fight or change the situation; such a choice is never a consideration. He faces his options and leaves. Time here is thus irreversible, non-cyclical. There is no going back. Whether the change ultimately involves only a shift in space and not a real transformation of the character is open to question. The text does not provide an answer. What the text does provide is a context for the heterogeneous voices gathered in Galindo's interviews. No longer disconnected nor out of context, these voices, alternating between gringos and chicanos, offer contrasting views of Jehú's personal affairs and in the process demystify the idyllic notion of community. Jehú's cynical view of himself and the community, shared by the interviewer Galindo, is best summed up as follows: "La raza es medio cabrona cuando quiere, and I'm fresh out of brotherly love. Los has de ver; (¿nos has de ver?). Hay poca vergüenza en este Valle."[32]

Rites and Witnesses

The book *Rites and Witnesses* is part of the *Mi querido Rafa* and *Korean Love Songs* sequence. In fact the text both precedes and parallels the time-frame in *Mi querido Rafa*. But while the latter offered a view of the ruling Anglo family from the perspective of Jehú and other Chicanos, *Rites* allows us to gain direct access to the private world of the KBC and, through their own English dialogue, become aware of their ambitions and biases.

Scenes of Rafa and other soldiers in the Korean battlefield are intercalated between the KBC dialogues. These Korean segments in dialogue form serve to elaborate information previously presented in verse form in *Korean Love Songs*. The juxtaposition of the two sets of dialogues, the two settings and the two time-frames (1960 in Klail City and 1950 in Korea) expresses the futility of the deaths of many American boys, among them many Chicanos whose bodies were fished out of the river by fellow soldiers so that the Klails, Blanchards and Cookes of the world could continue to profit, scheme, manipulate, fornicate and destroy the Valley of their forefathers. The Rites are for the dead in Korea and for the decaying Valley, in the hands of Anglo capitalists and their Chicano lackeys.

The second part of the book, "The Witnesses," is a series of testimonials by different citizens of Klail City, all Anglo except for one. Why these individuals testify about Mexicans in Klail City is not clear but these declarations appear to be a continuation of Galindo's interviews found in *Mi querido Rafa*. Most of the witnesses are older, the age of don Javier Leguizamón, and they express a variety of opinions; some praise assimilated and enterprising Mexicans like don Javier and Ira Escobar; others express their prejudice against Mexicans.

These testimonials also elaborate on previously presented information, providing now the Anglo perspective. Most of these Anglos are hispanicized and speak some Spanish; some married Mexicans; some are aware of the harrassment and murder perpetrated in the Mexican community by the Rangers and

Anglos; some are paternalistic; some totally disdainful and big-oted. Only one testimony from one of Jehú's and Rafa's class-mates comments specifically on Jehú's performance at the Bank. The final testimony is presented by Abel Manzano, a man of Echevarría's age, who provides information on Echevarría's ancestors and on the Texas Rangers' victimization of Mexicans in the early part of the 20th century.

It is this prejudice and victimization of Mexicans by the dominant Anglo society that is now juxtaposed with a continua-tion of the Korean War episodes. Like his ancestors, Rafa is exposed to death, now at the hands of an enemy he knows noth-ing about, but at the orders of Anglo commanders like Bracken, who instead of commending him for valor wants to court-martial him. In the battlefield there are bastards like Choche Markham, just as in the Valley. Here in battle, Chicano and Anglo youth interrelate in a way never seen in the Valley. Here the Anglo sol-diers are like brothers, whose deaths are as difficult for Rafa to accept as Chale Villalón's and Joey Vielma's from back home.

The sequence ends with an Army report of the attack which kills Joey and other members of Rafa's company; once again Rafa is wounded in action. It will be these old wounds which will take Rafa to a Veteran's hospital in *Mi querido Rafa.*

The novel ends with a cyclical repetitiveness, this time of death. As illusions die and idylls are seen to be non-existent, the characters are left with only a sense of loss and a view of life as simply a battle of wits and survival. But this anguish about life as a "death trip" is not stated in the novel. On the surface, the char-acters bed their women, attend barbecues and laugh. "There must be something else," is Jehú's cry. Perhaps in the next book, *Claros varones,* as the characters' personal lives intersect with history, they will find some answers.

---

[1]Rolando Hinojosa, *Estampas del valle y otras obras* (Berkeley: Quinto Sol Publications, 1973).

R. Hinojosa, *Generaciones y semblanzas* (Berkeley: Justa Publica-tions, 1979).

R. Hinojosa, *Korean Love Songs* (Berkeley: Justa Publications, 1978).

R. Hinojosa, *Mi querido Rafa* (Houston: Arte Público Press, 1981).

R. Hinojosa, *Rites and Witnesses* (Houston: Arte Público Press, 1982).

[2]Hinojosa, *Generaciones y semblanzas,* p. 1.

[3]Hinojosa, *Rites and Witnesses,* p. 8.

[4]M. M. Bakhtin, *The Dialogic Imagination* (Austin: U.T. Press, 1982), p. 261.

[5]Carlos Blanco Aguinaga, Julio Rodríguez Puértolas e Iris M. Zavala, *Historia social de la literatura española,* II (Madrid: Editorial Castalia), p. 103.

[6]*Ibid.*, I, p. 172.

[7]*Ibid.*

[8]*Ibid.*, p. 235.

[9]Erving Goffman, *Forms of Talk* (Philadelphia: University of Pennsylvania Press, 1981), p. 50.

[10]M. M. Bakhtin, *Estética de la creación verbal* (Mexico: Siglo Veintiuno Editores, 1982), p. 258.

[11]Hinojosa, *Generaciones y semblanzas,* p. 1.

[12]Arnoldo De León, *The Tejano Community 1836-1900* (Albuquerque: University of New Mexico Press, 1982), p. 14.

[13]Emilio Zamora, "Chicano Socialist Labor Activity in Texas, 1900-1920," in *Aztlán,* 6/2 (Summer 1975) p. 227.

[14]De León, pp. 18-19.

[15]*Ibid.*, p. 20.

[16]Hinojosa, *Generaciones y semblanzas,* p. 111.

[17]Gilberto Cárdenas, "Los desarraigados: Chicanos in the Midwest Region of the United States," in *Aztlán,* 7/2 (1976) pp. 153-186.

[18]Luis Rubalcava, "Mexican Migrant Workers in the Midwest: A Socio-Historical Perspective," in *Crítica,* 1/1 (1984), 49-78.

[19]Tomás Rivera, . . . *y no se lo tragó la tierra* (Berkeley: Quinto Sol Publications, 1971).

[20]Hinojosa, *Estampas,* pp. 133-134.

[21]Hinojosa, *Generaciones y semblanzas,* pp. 145-151.

[22]*Ibid.*

[23]*Ibid.*, p. 112.

[24]Bakhtin, *The Dialogic Imagination,* p. 263.

[25]Hinojosa, *Generaciones y semblanzas,* pp. 113 and 115.

[26]*Ibid.*, p. 13.

[27]Hinojosa, *Estampas,* p. 128.

[28]Bakhtin, *The Dialogic Imagination,* p. 162.

[29]*Ibid.*
[30]Hinojosa, *Mi querido Rafa*, p. 38.
[31]*Ibid.*, p. 50.
[32]*Ibid.*, p. 41.

Luis Leal
University of California, Santa Barbara

History and Memory in *Estampas del Valle*

A main preoccupation of the Chicano novelists of the Quinto Sol generation, the generation that was instrumental in bringing about the literary renaissance of the seventies, has been the validity of the regional tradition and its history. This obsession with cultural history was formulated by Américo Paredes in his essay "The Folk Base of Chicano Literature," in which he classified Chicano folklore into regional, rural, and urban. He illustrated his thesis with examples taken from frontier *corridos,* but he could very well have done it with any other genre. The culture found in the Valley, where Rolando Hinojosa's fiction takes place, belongs, according to Paredes' classification, to the regional type, a culture characterized by the presence of traits from Spain and Mexico which "have been kept alive for many generations" and upon which local adaptations have been made.[1] No less important is the fact that the space of that culture extends from Northern Mexico to the Valley, and its limits are "not defined by the Customs and Immigration offices at the border. Parts of northern Mexico are included within the boundaries of each. These regional folk cultures thus include regions of two nations" (p. 8).

Although Américo Paredes' definition is confined to the nature of the folk culture, the concept can be extended to include other aspects of life and literature. Hinojosa's world fits perfectly well within the definition of regional cultures as given by Paredes. The characters are descendants of the Spanish/Mexican settlers who arrived there during the eighteenth century. There they found themselves more isolated from the North American cultural tradition than the members of the other two groups, made up of recent arrivals of campesinos from Mexico who brought with them their rural traditions, and those who settled in the large urban centers, the latter tending to acculturate more readily. The inherited culture of Chicanos in urban centers has been modified to a larger extent than that of the other two groups, due mainly to the close proximity of cultures existing in the city. In the following pages I shall try to illustrate the nature of the regional culture in the novel *Estampas del valle y otras obras,*[2] although it permeates all of Hinojosa's fiction.

The Chicanos of the Valley where the action of the novel takes place have not lost their traditions or their cultural identity, and therefore they have a firm hold on the present. In that present time they relive the past, thus giving the novel a ritual structure. Experiences associated with death have left vivid memories on the mind of the narrator. At age thirty-four, that is, twenty-seven years later, he remembers the death of his mother: "I met death and its finality before I was quite seven years old" (p. 43). By association, he remembers another event that coincided with the later death of his father, the annual arrival of the maromeros (tumblers). In this manner the narrator reconstructs and keeps alive traditions which constitute a mosaic of experiences whose totality makes up life in the barrio. The vivid images make it possible for the reader acquainted with life on both sides of the border to relive that life, thus becoming conscious of a past which he thought had been lost forever:

> The circus consisted of a huge tent from which hung a trapeze, or from which they would stretch wires so that a girl in a bathing suit, or a man who pretended to be Japanese or drunk could balance on it, walking from one tip of the tent to the other. Generally there were four or five musicians who played from behind a little curtain that served as a backdrop for the rude stage where a clown or two, or sometimes the very same musicians, would present their show to the public. When the musicians made themselves up as clowns they would also sell little cardboard boxes of peanuts and hard candy in green, white and red stripes like the Mexican flag. (p. 43)

The train of thought about death, suddenly interrupted by the memory of the maroma, is recovered for a moment, only to be interrupted again by the dramatization of the narrator's visit to his Aunt Chedes. When he appears, she begins to cry, remembering the death of her brother. After she stops crying,

> (She) put her index finger to her mouth, placed the iron on the trivet and went to the icebox from which she brought me a glass of cold water. She stuck her middle finger in the glass, made the sign of the cross on my forehead and said, "Drink this down in one gulp while I say an Our Father Backwards" (44).

That ancient rite — cold water, middle finger, prayer said backward — serves to relive the mythical past, much alive for Aunt Chedes, but lost for the young narrator. His link with that past is provided by associating with relatives upon whom it still has a powerful influence. These liminal experiences (death of father, magic rite) are symbolic of a change towards a new social status on the part of the narrator, who is recapitulating that rite of passage.

Present actions bring to mind the past. The act of asking for the hand of a girl in marriage makes her father think about his own experience when he married, and he tries to imagine who the person was who gave away the hand of his wife's mother. In this manner the past is recovered and the simple action becomes a rite, the function of which is to recreate the past. The ritual nature of the act is repeated in the present, exactly as it had been done in the past.[3] Roque Malacara asks for the hand of Tere, and Tere's father, Jehú Vilches, remembers when he had asked don Braulio for Matilde's hand. Here history ends for Jehú, for he doesn't know who was the father of doña Sóstenes, Braulio's wife. "From the threshold I catch a glimpse of my deceased father-in-law, don Braulio Tapia, with his drooping mustache and long sideburns, greeting me just like when I came here to ask for Matilde. By that time, he had already lost his wife, doña Sóstenes, just as I've lost Matilde. Don Braulio says yes, shakes my hand and lets me come in. Whom did don Braulio see at the threshold when he asked for his wife?" (p. 40). Later on, the narrator reconstructs the life history of the Tapia family. "Braulio appeared in what is now Belken County in 1908 and two years later married Sóstenes Calvillo, the only daughter of don Práxedis Calvillo and Albinita Buenrostro. From this marriage came Matilde; she married Jehú Vilches and they had a daughter, María Teresa de Jesús, who married Roque Malacara" (p. 127).

√ The narrator functions as the historical conscious of a regional society that has not had the fortune of having a written history. He remembers the lives of all the inhabitants of the barrio and their participation in historical events. Braulio Tapia, born in El Esquilmo (now Skidmore), Texas, in August of 1883, was brought up by Juan Nepomuceno Celaya and a maternal aunt, both from Goliad, Texas, "where the person who replaced General Urrea executed Colonel Fannin and the other rebels during the rebellion of Texas in 1835-36" (p. 127).

By broadening the perspective from individual to family, to county, to state, Hinojosa skillfully presents the total historical development of a regional culture along the border. While reconstructing a family tree, the narrator introduces events of significance in the formation of the new social status of the Mexican in the Valley. The relationship of the characters to the land joins the past and the present and gives continuity to the unfolding of their history:

> Arriving at this last generation, the lands and properties that la raza owned in the area already belonged, for the most part, to the Anglos: la raza that managed to keep their lands could almost be divided into two categories: first, the older generation who banded together against the Anglos in "logrolling" deals (although blood was also shed); and secondly, the rest, those that were covetous, that is, la raza who sided with the Anglos in order to eat up the leftovers in the form of land that rebels, politicians and lawyers left to them (p. 127).

Braulio Tapia also has the function of linking the history of Mexico to that of the Valley, thus giving cultural unity to that region found along both sides of the Río Grande. He remembers his experiences as a participant in the Mexican Revolution. He belongs, as do Evaristo Garrido and don Manuel Guzmán, to a generation whose members in Belken County are "getting scarce." They remember stories about the Mexican Revolution, for they fought in the armies of Pancho Villa and Lucio Blanco. Memory, at times, may be unfaithful to some of the inhabitants of Belken County, especially the older generation (Don Braulio Tapia can't remember how many bullets he has in his body), but not to the narrator, who reconstructs their lives and gives them a history, a reconstructed history. When the few old revolutionaries who are not in nursing homes get together at night at the bench on the corner "and gab about this and that," they re-tell the same stories, mostly about their adventures in the armies of Villa and Lucio Blanco. Those stories, however, change every time they are told, for the memory of the storytellers, "that unfaithful lover, trips them up from time to time" (p. 126). Thus, their stories become creative narratives that feed their imagination and that of the inhabitants of the barrio, however unreliable they may be to the professional historian.

The narrator, likewise, rescues from forgetfulness past experiences which constitute an important aspect of the human history of Belken County, and that historical reconstruction is accomplished just in time, for some of the revolutionaries and members of older generations no longer recall the details. Braulio fought at San Pedro de las Colonias, but the memory is fading:

> San Pedro de las Colonias;
> qué lejos te vas quedando
> ¡quedando!
> (San Pedro de las Colonias
> You're getting further away,
> further and further away —)

The histories of Northern Mexico and the Valley in Texas are hard to keep as two separate entities. The Valley was settled by people who came from Mexico with José de Escandón (1700-1770), the founder of Nuevo Santander, now the state of Tamaulipas. He brought from Querétaro numerous settlers during the middle of the eighteenth century and founded twenty-one communities and several missions. Among those settlers was the Buenrostro family, prominent in *Estampas,* as were the Lerdos: "Los Lerdo came to the Valley with los Buenrostro when don José de Escandón dazzled half the world in Querétaro" (p. 132). Ties with Mexico are not broken after 1836, as families and individuals keep coming and going across the imaginary border. The Leguizamón family, for instance, "arrived in Belken County in 1865, johnny-come-latelies, so to speak, and established themselves in what is now Bascom and part of Flora"(132). As late as the early nineteenth century the descendants of the original Buenrostro make a trip to Mexico, "during those fierce dog days of 1904, a year when it didn't rain a single day in Belken County. (That same year, seven wagons replete with people, rosaries and provisions, left Klail City and Edgerton toward San Juan de los Lagos, Jalisco, to pray to the Virgin for rain in Belken. Julián Buenrostro, Jesús *El quieto's* younger brother, was born on this trip)" (p. 132).

This close relationship between chicanos "de este lado" and Mexicanos "del otro lado" is summarized with these words:

> These old men like don Braulio Tapia, Evaristo Garrido and don Manuel Guzmán, were born in the US but fought in the Revolution as so many others of the same age and breed. The parents of these men were also born in this country as were their grandparents (and here we are referring to 1765 and before). To the Mexican-American, the land was all the same, given the proximity to the border and the mess of relatives on both sides who never distinguished between the land and the river, but crossed the one and the other as if it were one and the

same. It was always like that and even though the immigration service — la migra — doesn't believe so, it continues being the same for many Mexican Americans today. (p. 126)

This uninterrupted relationship with Mexico has made it possible for the inhabitants of the Valley to keep their cultural traditions almost intact. Among the many traditions of popular origin still present is the use of the *corrido* or popular ballad as a mnemotechnic device to help them remember important events, in the absence of a written history. The novelist makes use of this imporant source of information to reconstruct the history of the Chicanos of the Valley. As in several Latin American novels, there is in *Estampas* an accident caused by a railroad derailment. The event was sung in a *corrido* well known in the Valley:

> Beto's parents died in an accident in Flora when a freight train killed some twenty people, among them, Beto's parents. (In less than a week, los Ayala had written a corrido that became a hit among la raza. The Acosta publishing company printed it and Barrientos set it to music. The record was cut by Aguila Records in Corpus Christi.) The family, Beto included, was on its way to the fields when their truck stalled on the tracks and that's when the deaths occurred. (p. 134)

In general it can be said that among the members of this border regional community Mexican culture predominates. However, after a century of interaction with the Anglo-American culture some acculturation, however slight, has taken place. At the *maroma* the vendors sell foods, most of them of Mexican origin, such as *charamuscas, calabazates, dulces de leche quemada*; but they also sell American products, like *sodas* y *leche malteada*. Most important, to drink the *sodas* a private *popote* (drinking straw) is provided for reasons of personal hygiene. These bicultural images are not frequent in *Estampas,* as the Mexican images predominate; however, they do appear at regular intervals to create the right milieu of the region, where contact between the two cultures leads to some acculturation.

Roque Malacara and his wife Tere have a son who is so like his grandfather that his father thinks, "If people are reborn, I'd say that my son and his granddad are the same person" (p. 42). By inheriting the features and acquiring the cultural characteristics of their forebears, the people of Belken County continue the traditions handed down from the past and, at the same time, transmit them to future generations. The technique utilized by the narrator is that of memory, for by means of memory it is possible for the characters to recall at regular intervals events in their lives and in the lives of other inhabitants of the Valley, thus giving the novel a pattern of historical time.

The verbal structure of *Estampas del Valle* reflects the regional nature of the culture that still prevails in the Valley. This verbal structure describes life, customs, mores, and traditions in Belken County, a county representative of those along the Rio Grande in the State of Texas. The images, metaphors and similes around which the novel is structured give the work its validity, for it is a satisfactory set of verbal symbols for the world it describes. By means of these verbal symbols Hinojosa *ha rescatado* the regional culture of the Chicano of Klail City, Condado de Belken, Valle del Río Grande, y sus alrededores.

---

[1]Américo Paredes, "The Folk Base of Chicano Literature," in Joseph Sommers and Tomás Ybarra-Frausto, *Modern Chicano Writers* (Englewood Cliffs, N.J.: Prentice-Hall, 1979), p. 8.

[2]Rolando Hinojosa, *Estampas del valle y otras obras. Sketches of the Valley and Other Works.* English trans. by Gustavo Valadez and José Reyna (Berkeley, California: Editorial Justa Publications, 1973). Page numbers in the text refer to the second printing, 1977.

[3]There is a variant here, for Roque has no sponsors to accompany him, a necessary part of the ceremony. However Jehú is conscious of the fact and thinks, "'What can I do?' — he doesn't have any sponsors and that's why he comes all by himself to ask me for Tere's hand" (p. 40).

Yolanda Julia Broyles
University of Texas at San Antonio

Hinojosa's *Klail City y sus alrededores*:
Oral Culture and Print Culture

No Chicano literary work has received more international recognition and less scholarly attention than Rolando Hinojosa-Smith's *Generaciones y semblanzas* (1977), first published under the title *Klail City y sus alrededores* (1976). *Klail City* won the most distinguished and coveted literary prize of Latin America, the Premio Casa de las Américas (1976). Only two years after its initial publication it found its way into the Eastern bloc, via the German Democratic Republic: a Volk & Welt edition entitled *Klail City und Umgebung*.[1] In recognition of the novel's merits, the Federal Republic of Germany's premier publisher, Suhrkamp Verlag, adopted the East German edition for publication in the West.[2] The publisher's only problem was whether to market the work as part of the Latin American program or part of the United States literature program. In the United States, the Chicano publishing company Justa Publications (now defunct) solved the problem by means of a bilingual Spanish/English edition.[3] Indeed, the novel's firm footing in both Latin American literature and United States literature defies the arbitrary political borders and the corresponding categories of national literatures. *Klail City* is a prime example of the type of Chicano literature which is *sin fronteras*. It is born as the spiritual, political and economic intersection of the Anglo and the Mexican worlds.

Although *Klail City* has found a wide international audience, it appears to be passing into oblivion among Chicano readers and critics. As incomprehensible as it might seem, *Klail City* has been out of print for some time now in the United States, with no new edition in sight. Among critics, *Klail City* has only inspired a dozen short reviews and one sustained essay in the eight years since its publication.[4] This dearth of critical reflection upon Hinojosa's seminal work is particularly startling in view of the explosion of critical response that other major Chicano novels have triggered. As we witness a constant increase of writings on Rudolfo Anaya's *Bless Me, Ultima* or Tomás Rivera's *y no se lo tragó la tierra*, we also witness the marginalization of other works and even areas of inquiry. Why has *Klail City y sus alredededores*, Hinojosa's pivotal work, not generated more of a critical response?

Answers to that question will crystallize in the course of the present exploration of *Klail City*. What I advance is one view of that text, based on a textual examination, on observations of mexicano/chicano life in Texas, and on theoretical considerations which I will outline. This essay is intended as a stimulus to readers and critics. In no way do I consider my own vision of *Klail City y sus alredededores* definitive or exhaustive. The complexity of the work — and the variety of perspectives we can bring to bear upon it — could conceivably generate a multitude of interpretations. Yet present limitations of space necessarily entail restrictions in my treatment of the work. I restrict myself to a discussion of what I consider to be the basis of Hinojosa's narrative strategy and narrative power: community and the communal culture of orality.

Community in 'Klail City'

The very titles of Hinojosa's novels convey collectivity: *Klail City y sus alredededores* and *Generaciones y semblanzas*. These collective nouns in the plural at once span numerous times (generaciones), spaces (Klail City y sus alredededores) and agents (semblanzas). Both of Hinojosa's titles imply a broad scope, unlike the scores of Chicano titles which reveal a reduced, particularistic, often individualistic, primary focus: *Barrio Boy*; *Autobiography of a Brown Buffalo*; *Bless Me, Ultima*; *y no se lo tragó la tierra*; *Pocho*. Where these works do include community, it is filtered through the experiences of the protagonist.

There is another significant dimension to the title: *Generaciones y semblanzas* is freely borrowed from Fernán Pérez de Guzmán, Castillian chronicler of the deeds of Spanish nobility. The preface to the fourteenth century *Generaciones y semblan-*

zas reflects upon the proper way of depicting "los poderosos reyes e notables príncipes e grandes cibdades" in "high style": "e aya buena retórica para poner la estoria en fermoso e alto estilo."[5] With fine irony Hinojosa subverts that lofty tradition of writing which glorifies powerholders. He speaks of persons engaged in common activities ranging from the more profane level of going to the bathroom to the metaphysical plane of Chicano steadfastness, *no rajarse*: "Aquí no hay héroes de leyenda: esta gente va al escusado, estornuda, se limpia los mocos, cría familias, conoce lo que es morir con el ojo pelón, se cuartea con dificultad y (como madera verde) resiste rajarse."[6] Hinojosa's rhetorical styles are completely unlike the Castillian chronicler, as well. Throughout the novel we hear in place of the "alto estilo" a vivid vernacular ("morir al ojo pelón").

The concept of "heroism" is also turned on its head by Hinojosa. Living the day-to-day, surviving, facing up to "whatever life brings" ("lo que la vida depare") are deemed heroic, and certainly more courageous and impressive than the isolated grandiose single acts: "La gente sospecha que el vivir es algo heroico en sí." Daily *aguante* (enduring) is at the basis of the heroism of *Klail City*. Those readers expecting notables of the glorious-warrior type are admonished to look elsewhere.

The preface to *Klail City* postulates a vision of a world not of outstanding individuals nor even of any particular individuals, but of the daily life and death processes in which human beings are involved: "la gente que. . . . nace y grita también llora y ríe y va viviendo como puede. . .. al fin, todos mueren." Significantly, the protagonists are all grouped in a collective noun: "esta gente," "la gente." The heroic virtue of *aguante* is even said to be acquired in that group context: ". . . el aguante le viene a uno como consecuencia del forcejeo diario con el prójimo." This focus on communality and shared experience anticipates the contours of the narrative text that follows. Those contours, we are told, will emerge through the spoken words of common people: "entre diálogos y monólogos." Thus we are introduced to the ends (generaciones y semblanzas) and the means (diálogos y monólogos) of Hinojosa's prose fiction. What are the narrative techniques through which the community of Klail City (Belken County) is expressed?

Words: Orality and Print

The presence of orality and of elements from the oral tradition within Chicano literature is often mentioned in passing. Yet the inventory of forms peculiar to Chicano oral culture has not received the necessary attention from literary scholars, nor has their strong presence within Chicano print culture been adequately explored. It is the analysis of written texts which dominates all manner of institutional learning, while oral forms and the traditional dynamics of orality which inform much of our creative use of language have been relegated to special categories of marginalization reserved for indigenous cultures: folklore or anthropology. Chicanos passing through those institutions have often internalized the academic paradigms of print culture and literacy to the point of losing all but the most vague memory of the oral Mexican traditions which have formed the core of our culture throughout the millenia. That loss might also partially explain the apparent disregard for Hinojosa's *Klail City y sus alrededores,* a work firmly planted in the soil of community and oral culture.

A brief description of what is meant by "oral culture" and orality is in order. The terms "orality" and "oral culture" are not merely references to "talk" or to spoken language. Rather, they encompass a form of human consciousness, a person's relationship to the surrounding organic world, a way of life. In oral cultures virtually all forms of human action happen in conjunction with verbal forms of exchange. Words have a physical presence, they are created by the human body, received aurally, and they are directly relevant to a lived set of circumstances. Printed words, however, exist separate from any living context in which they might have been created; they are not embedded in human movement. As such they can soar to platonic levels of abstraction and self-reflection; there is no listener to take you at your word. This fact is reflected in the German popular saying: "Papier ist geduldig." "Paper is patient" in the sense of long-suffering. Words in oral cultures do possess a concreteness and meaning lost to words which are mass produced through the technology of print, electronic word processing, advertising, media and other branches of the consciousness industry.

The meaning of locutions in oral cultures is of a communal nature. Participation in these forms — such as cuentos, albures, cábula, corridos, rancheras, boleros, alabanzas, pastorelas, oraciones — has the effect of spiritual integration; it ties the individual in. Walter Ong notes: "Primary orality fosters personality structures that in certain ways are more communal and externalized, and less introspective than those common among literates. Oral communication unites people in groups. Writing and reading are solitary activities that throw the psyche back on itself."[7] In Chicano communities the transmission of history, for example, frequently happens verbally and in groups through the communal singing of *corridos,* or through the voice of an elder's recollection. The human bonding that comes of joking and other humor reaches a high degree of sophistication in structured forms of verbal dueling such as albures, choteo, or cábula; virtuosity in the practice of insult or flattery (or one of these in the form of the other) also has its patterns. Emotional experiences are frequently channeled through communal genres of oral lyricism, such as the *ranchera,* the *bolero,* or the *son.* Popular sentiment concerning a wide range of topics often is crystallized through the popular verses of a *declamador* or *declamadora.* Those verses are often transmitted through many generations by memory; others are improvised on the spot at family celebrations or other community gatherings. A repertoire of children's rhymes, songs and games unite them in play activities. Through oral traditions we are connected — if we so choose — to the world of our parents, grandparents and of our children, through human memory. Print culture, on the other hand, fosters intertextuality, but not direct living interpersonal relations. Persons immersed in print culture by virtue of university or other training, of course, continue to use the spoken word. Yet it is not comparable to the oral concept of "buen hablar"; nor do their oral skills display the range of imagination and improvisational dexterity found among strongly oral populations. It can hardly surprise us that the highly regarded quality of being "bien educado" in Chicano culture refers to a certain graciousness in interpersonal dealings, and not to formal schooling in any sense of literacy.

In spite of the power of the print industries — and others based on print — Chicano forms from the oral tradition have shown remarkable resilience, partially in response to foreign domination.[8] Publisher Nicolás Kanellos has stated: "We have not rediscovered the power of the word in declamation in its tribal and authentic setting; we never lost it."[9]

Orality in 'Klail City'

The narrative techniques employed in *Klail City* are not for the most part derived from the repository of written fiction conventions. They are anchored in spoken language forms; they are drawn from the storehouse of spoken language and human relationships found in tight-knit settings such as the community of Belken County. The "dialogues and monologues" announced by the narrator convey a multiplicity of voices encompassing various generations and a staggering number of different characters and situations. These dialogues and monologues span seemingly disparate elements such as Casa de Putas, North Ward, Korea, Don Efraín, Una Carta, Pa' Indiana, El Accidente. Yet they are not as discrete as they might appear. The unifying feature is that they are sketches of a generic nature, exemplary of patterns and forms of Mexican/Chicano oral culture.

Esteban Echevarría, for example, is the voice of collective memory. Historical memory is transmitted through verbal performance, not through written materials. Events of significance in the Mexicano community are the guideposts of Echevarría's narrative. His dramatic and emotive narrative in the bar El Oasis recounts the violence perpetrated by rinches (Texas Rangers) and the gullibility of *raza*. It is a subversive history for it contradicts the official Anglo record upheld by the courts, and disseminated in history books. Echevarría also is the voice of wisdom dispelling stereotyped notions such as that of the femme fatale: "Ella (Sóstenes) no tenía que ver nada en el asunto. Ah, ¿y después? Ah, pos la raza decía que por la culpa de las mujeres. . . . ¡Raza pendeja! Se mataron por pendejos."[10] *Los ancianos* (elders), men and women like Echevarría, exist in all Chicano communities. They preserve and transmit the experiences and memories which are the history and culture of a community. Echevarría's words of remembrance and recollection constitute a speech act possible only in a communication situation with others to whom he transmits, among other things, the historical record in its popular medium of expression: "La bolillada se cree que los rinches son gallones — me cago en los rinches y en sus pinches fundas contoy pistolas" (p. 11). Echevarría serves not to demonstrate individuality or any uniqueness of character but to illustrate and reinforce what is communal. He does that through *la palabra* (the word).

If the medium of exchange in an oral culture is talk, the value of speech depends on the worth of words. In strongly oral cultures — such as those of Mexican borderland communities — language resonates with respect for the word: *cortar la palabra; pedir la palabra; tener la palabra*; or, above all, *tener palabra.* These words carry a vital meaning unknown within cultures of literacy in which the inflationary industrial production of words (in print and other media) has eviscerated both their meaning and their value. The English equivalents of *cortar la palabra, tener la palabra* and *tener palabra* ignore the *word*: "we are cut off," "we have the floor," "we have honor." When English does ascribe value to words, as in "He/she kept his/her word" it is only of relative value, relative to him/her. *La palabra,* at once general and specific, conveys notions of honor and worth in a way which English has seen only at the beginning of *The Gospel according to St. John. Echevarría tiene la palabra,* the phrase which introduces Echevarría in the novel, does not mean merely that it is Echevarría's turn to talk. It means that he deserves the listeners' respect and attention, for the word he bears is the vessel of his community's history, its commonality. In the case of Echevarría, that community is *raza* of the Rio Grande Valley of South Texas, ("El Valle"/"The Valley"), a strongly oral region.

Another "generic" speech act in *Klail City* is the sales pitch for bibles performed by Jehú Malacara (assistant to the itinerant protestant preacher, Tomás Imás). The sales pitch is intimately related to the *sermón aleluya,* whose practitioners and participants can be found throughout Texas. The speech acts of Chicano protestantism have little in common with Echevarría's at the level of rhetorical devices and philosophical thrust. Yet as genres from oral culture they are functionally related: both oral performances constitute community events which link human beings into a unified group through the persuasive use of language. Jehú's sale of English language Bibles to Spanish speakers who do not know English requires considerable verbal skill. Jehú Malacara shows himself a master of that skill so highly prized in oral culture: verbal improvisation. He compensates for his lack of familiarity with the Bible, for example, through frequent, random Biblical quotations, which he quickly weaves into the flow of his sales pitch, bending and breaking their meaning without hesitation: "como dice el buen santo Deuteronomio."[11] In his verbal resourcefulness he appeals to people in the alluring style of a fortune-teller or palmist: "¿Tiene usted pregunta? ¿Tiene usted mala suerte? ¿El amor de una persona especial? La respuesta la encontrará allí en este libro sagrado." His manipulative verbal acrobatics anticipate the listeners' disinterest in an English language Bible: "¿Qué no leen inglés? ¿Y qué? Leyendo las santas palabras del viejo — digo y repito — viejo y viejísimo testamento será lo suficiente para sentirse salvados. ¡El poder de la palabra escrita!" The deep irony and *picardía* of this final statement becomes even clearer as Jehú proceeds to tell his listeners that *owning* the book is sufficient for salvation. One needn't understand what one reads ("¡Qué milagro, gente! ¿Me oyen?"). In this and other segments of the novel, Jehú recalls his time spent with the Carpa Peláez. We may be sure that his apprenticeship in the carpa — an itinerant tent show highlighting various forms of raucous entertainment — sharpened his verbal skills in improvised monologues.

The partnership between Jehú Malacara and Brother Tomás Imás briefly highlights another domain of oral culture: the communal activity of song. As Tomás Imás and Jehú Malacara dialogue about singing hymns, Jehú learns that "El vals *Paloma mensajera vuela y dile (a la que amando espero)* del maestro Olivares tiene la mismísima tonada que dos de los himnos favoritos del hermano Imás, a saber, *Inocente pastor cuida a tu rebaño* y *Pon tu mano sacra en esa llaga*" (p. 135). The simple facts explained by Jehú — that he learned songs from his father, that his father "era lírico," and that Tomás Imás' protestant hymn tunes were originally tunes from popular songs — illustrate three major traits of oral lyricism: the transmission of sung texts from generation to generation ("mi papá lo tocaba en el acordeón"), their transmission through memory and not through musical notation ("era lírico"), and the process by which sung texts undergo adaptation and transformation as they are passed down.

The presence of a rich and varied body of traditional song forms in the Chicano community is echoed and reinforced throughout *Klail City.* Passing references to a number of different forms of oral lyricism punctuate the text. For instance, the corrido of Ambrosio Mora (murdered in cold blood by a *rinche*) is referred to by Echevarría. Later it appears one line at a time interspersed within the dialogues and monologues that relate the circumstances of his death; each corrido line is set apart as if to represent a capsule of collective memory in the process of crystallization. Other references are to the tango (of Argentine proletarian origin and Mexican by adoption), and the paso doble, *Silverio Perez,* by Augustın Lara.

A long-standing institution of Chicano oral culture in rural, semi-rural, and urban areas is the *locutor*: the radio announcer, or "DJ," whose disembodied voice fills homes, shops, cars, many public places and work places. In *Klail City* that voice belongs to Enedino Broca López, "La voz del pueblo, con el pueblo, y para el pueblo" (p. 153). Many famous *locutores* emerged from the oral tradition of the *carpas*. Most famous among them was Tin-Tan, who later worked in film as well. Beloved and even legendary *locutores* in Chicano communities, such as Martín Rosales (KGET, Harlingen), Genaro Tamez (KWBU, Corpus Christi), José López "El relámpago" (formerly KEDA, San Antonio), or Pedro J. Gonzalez (Los Angeles) are those who have successfully functioned as "transmitters" of widespread public sentiment channeled to them through the community. It is a strongly personalized "voice of a friend" ("su locutor amigo") whose every word aims to please and uplift. A good voice, prodigious verbal dexterity and charm are basic requirements for good radio performance. Enedino Broca López' performance establishes close communication with the community ("el amable radioescucha", p. 151) through a constant flow of musical dedications, greetings, messages, and other forms of direct address. Maintaining the listeners' attention even through commercials, of course, requires special vocal effects involving changes in volume, pitch, rhythm, inflection and intonation: "pero primero, UNos ANUNcios de unas de las casas que PATROcinan éste" (p. 155). Enedino's intentional or unintentional word juggling also creates hilarious and risqué double entendres: ". . . Kirby Brothers donde tienen gangas en ropa interior — han bajado — los precios" (p. 155). Occasionally profanity escapes his lips: "riata chingao" (p. 151). It is the general playfulness, good cheer and sharp wit which are at the basis of the *locutor's* special powers in the community, powers born of *la palabra*. The speech acts of *locutores* constitute a counterpoint to Echevarría's gravity. By inverting seriousness into fine mockery and play, the *locutor* lightens spirits. Laughter releases — even if momentarily — the tension of problems, the burden of daily human struggles. Enedino Broca López represents the remarkable function of *locutores* or other agents of humor within strongly oral cultures.

The use of oral cultural forms as narrative techniques in *Klail City* almost blurs one's consciousness of them as "narrative techniques." We are invaded by a feeling that the townspeople are in truth speaking for themselves instead of being narrated. That feeling is heightened through the absence of an anonymous narrator of the detached and omniscient sort. Narration by Jehú Malacara or Rafa Buenrostro, for example, contains clear indicators of their involvement in whatever they narrate. In addition to the longer types of generic monologues, short forms are also applied. These include *choteo* and *cábula,* favorite forms of verbal jousting requiring considerable linguistic resources and alertness. The varied techniques of *cábula* include puns, all manner of allusions, role-playing and role-switching, mockery, irony, and a constant savoring and manipulation of the physical constitution of spoken words: their sounds and rhythm. One dialogue concerning Clementina, Enedino Broca López' companion, demonstrates some of these elements:

> No pendejo, el Enedino quiere quedar bien con la Clementina hija única (algo feíta, eso sí) y. . .
> Fea con "efe" de ¿fundillo?
> Bueno, es m s bien fea-fea; no es fea-fea-fea-fea, ¿me entiende?
> Entonces no es fea con "efe" de . . .
> No; y además tiene sus centavos.
> Ah, ya. . . con eso basta.
> Pues, sí, es riquita de dineros que no de cueros.
> Eso ya se dijo.
> Sí, pero no de esa manera (p. 153).

In reference to the miserly nature of Clementina's father, a passerby adds: "¡Qué va! Si es mas apretado que culo de perra en brama . . ." (p. 133).

The inexhaustible richness of Chicano everyday oral expression unfolds through numerous short dialogues concerning the daily events of life. They illustrate various types of conversational exchange patterns. Spoken forms are in some instances presented with phonetic authenticity: "Shsta, h'mbre" (p. 3l); "Cho gusto" (p. 29); "pa' 'lla vamos"   *Klail City* encompasses a variety of Chicano speech   ingular to Chicano literature. We encounter all mann   s, including a storehouse of earthbound metaphoric   ....ption ("era un garañón de potrero El Pioquinto", p. 133), the folk wisdom of dichos ("el que la busca la encuentra", p. 167), profanities of conventional and less conventional sorts; formulaic expressions ("de cabo a rabo" or "con una mano adelante y otra atras", p. 161), all manner of slang and other verbal inventiveness. One of the most remarkable features in *Klail City* is the fine sense of irony and affectionate mockery sustained throughout the novel.

Hinojosa's fondness for the spoken word and his desire to showcase its forms with verisimilitude lead him at one point to render two simultaneous conversations on the printed page, as if to overcome the unrelenting rectilinear thrust of written words — of course, we see the two conversations side by side, but we cannot read them simultaneously. In a strongly oral culture, locutions are not linear but circular: spoken words happen in many places at the same and at different times, but they recur. They return from mouth to mouth to revive a life experience, an event. Those that recur most often find a generic form and become community. They recur in *Klail City* where townsfolk recollect them. The medium is memory and the instrument is voice. Memory both constitutes and transmits culture. The crucial significance of memory in the text is underscored through a rare authorial intervention in the world of Klail City:

> El que esto escribe (así como los que escriben otras cosas) teme olvidar algo que en un tiempo fue muy importante para él. . . . El que esto escribe también cree mucho en eso de cambiar de dirección (una de sus

más nuevas creencias) y, quizá por eso, también cree que al hacerlo ha recobrado algo que, impensable e insensiblemente, iba gastando: el recuerdo de ser quién, qué y de dónde es (p. 101).

The recurrence of communally significant words, that revival of an experience comes through acts of recollection that are, for example, inherent to corridos as they are sung, to stories as they are told and re-told, as they "circulate." Memory coils and spirals. The circularity of spoken words is embedded in various *Klail City* narrative sections. The human ties involved in the path of the spoken word are revealed also through frequent oral-aural markers such as:

> *contaba* Doña Herminia. . . .
> *Por Esteban Echevarría se supo* más tarde. . . .
> En otro lugar, y en otra ocasion *se contó*. . . .
> Cuando a Julián Buenrostro *le avisaron*. . . .
> *Tú lo has dicho.* (all p. 23)

Another feature of oral circularity is apparent in the common conversational feature of repeating what the previous person has said before responding. That repetition forms a physical and mental link with the others' spoken words. For example, in the dialogue of the two compadres:

> ¿Y si no llueve compadre?
> Pos si no llueve se jodió la burra.
> Y la mula.
> Y la mula y el tomate.
> Y fíjese que pensaba emparejarme con el tomate, compadre.
>
> Que se cuide el que se atreva. . .
> Eso, que se cuide, sí señor.

Similarly, in the comadres' dialogue:

> Pero es que nunca falta.
> Verda . . . si no es esto es lo otro o algo más allá.
> Eso . . . es que nunca falta . . . (p. 143)

It is the network of orality that gives the novel its ~~~~ ness.

Spirals or concentric circles of spoken w~~~~ itute themselves around events at the time those events happen and later as they are recalled. One of the main narrative features of *Klail City* is that type of verbal recurrence. We follow some events as they happen, as they are told, retold, or as they recur in a parenthetical mention. For example, there are five sections which revolve around Enedino Broca López; the marriage of Jovita de Anda and Joaquín Tamez is variously echoed: we are told about the Tamez brothers intermittently and from different points of view; the circumstances surrounding the accidental death of Esteban and Dorotea Muzquiz are spoken from four different perspectives; Don Jesús Buenrostro is revealed to us the first time through Echevarría's recollection of that man's murder; again the night it happens; again in the form of a story about how his brother avenged his murder; through various evocations of "El Quieto." Times, people, events are rearranged in kaleidoscopic manner. Instead of broken reflections we have the spiraling of spoken words through time and space.

The power of the spoken word as a connector between past, present and future, as a living unifying force among people, as the medium in which community comes together is foregrounded in *Klail City*. Speech acts are the threads with which the social fabric of Belken County is woven. Through *la palabra* an existential web of recurring forms of human interaction is revealed. Belken County's eloquent self-narration, the prominence of oral forms has far-reaching ramifications for various narrative elements traditionally considered to be pillars of narrative.[12] Elements such as plot, character and setting are felicitously minimized or reduced to vestigial organs. It would, for example, be impossible to describe a plot or any neat sequence of events in *Klail City*. Any description of what happens, of story line, would break into as many segments as there are in the novel. Also, the sheer number of different speakers in the novel makes it difficult to neatly order all we are told. Indeed, the novel's constant changes of place, time, and characters disrupt the type of expansive narrational flow that would allow for some traditional narrative features, such as character development, the unfolding of a unified plot, or sustained description of any sort. Instead of narrational flow we encounter episodic mini-segments with no linear progression, nor homogeneous story line. The segments of mundane events do not combine to form a plot; rather they constitute interlocking circles. We had been alerted to that in the preface: "Este mundo de Belken County es un ir y venir . . . unos suben y otros bajan . . . . y al llegar la hora de la hora, *aquí no ha pasado nada*" (emphasis mine) p. 1. Plot as an organizing element is minimized. The many segments in *Klail City* become mutually entailing through recurring voices highlighting the word in the community and the community in the word.

Individual bearers of these voices are not physically described by any third-person voice nor by each other. In a sense, Hinojosa's characters are indistinguishable from the speech acts they perform. We are given no physical description of Echevarría or of anyone else. We learn of each character only that part of them by which they are linked to others through an oral performance. Characters are means rather than ends unto themselves. They exist primarily in their relationship to the community and not as standard-bearers of individualism. Interestingly, that strong bond to the community in no way compels them to be of the synthetic and prosaic "representative" sort. To the contrary, they are all eccentric.

Nothing could be further from Hinojosa's narrative strategy than a concern with individualism or personal crises so pervasive in modern western writing.[13] In *Klail City* there is no peering into individual psyches; there are no "round" characters, no internal psychological growth, no introspection. The individual self is not an organizing principle. The work's narrative devices ingeniously parallel the reality of life in a community based in oral culture. Hinojosa's narrative techniques in *Klail C* reflect the interdependence, not independence, o   ings. Characters are constituted not as much throug   g for the separateness of individuality but through   ario con el prójimo" (p. 1). Neither Echevarría, nor Jehu, nor Elledino Broca López speak in order to reveal private feelings or their personality. Their speech acts bespeak community. Hinojosa's minimization of individual character counters the tendency in modern fiction toward individual uniqueness as well as that penchant toward individual protagonists *qua* representative characters which abound in Chicano literature. Hinojosa's *Klail City* even appears to call into question the existence of "representative characters." What appears to be representative are the cultural forms of talk, the commonly held cultural molds of oral communication which are fleshed out or temporarily embodied by this or that character. We can be sure that Echevarría's oral performance genre is a cultural constant and will be repeated many times over, although not necessarily by him.

In rendering the spoken word in print, Hinojosa has eliminated various conventions of written narrative used to set off spoken language. No quotation marks are used in dialogues. No tags are used to identify speakers. No transitional remarks help orient us in the constant shift from past to future to present, from one point of view to another. Each segment begins abruptly in midstream. The absence of such novelistic markers creates an absorbing immediacy, which immerses us in the discourse of the community. But like participants in oral communication we are forced to adjust quickly to a changing context. From readers Hinojosa demands a mental faculty indispensible to participants in oral culture: a strong presence of mind and the corresponding agility of response.

Setting in *Klail City* is also of particular interest. Those who read the novel learn nothing of the physical appearance of the

Rio Grande Valley. There are no descriptions of places that portray the town of Klail City or other towns. Yet the settings mentioned are by no means gratuitous background locations which function as foils. Places repeatedly mentioned in Klail City are of a particular type: they are public and not private spaces. They are the communal spaces where people congregate, the spaces that require speech, which is the living breath of exchange. The park benches, sidewalks and streetcorners variously mentioned in the novel, are vortices of verbal exchange. Other such locales of community in Klail City are the bar, whorehouse, schools, plazita, the cemetery, the trucks carrying farmworkers north, even the Korean battlefields where Klail City youth meet. What is memorable in the novel is not a unified plot, nor any intricacies of narration, nor character development. Klail City, Belken County, the Chicano population of the Rio Grande Valley is unveiled as a social web possessing a common past and present preserved and enacted in the word, in the oral acts of cultural preservation. That is the thrust of lived culture in South Texas. But it also lives — to varying degrees — in Chicano communities throughout the United States.[14] Rolando Hinojosa has commented:

> No se trata ya ni nunca de una región sino de un modo de pensar de mucha gente. . . . Se escribe de una región, de historias particulares, pero el lector, ese de Detroit y aquel otro de Guadalajara, ve que no se trata de esa región sino de la suya, y el Valle será el de Texas cercano al Golfo, pero otros lo ven al Valle como el de ellos, el de San Luis, o el Imperial, el Yakima el Willamette, y así. No hay que particularizar: la gente sabe de quién se habla.[15]

In addition to considerations of narrative plot, setting, characters and the relationship to readers, a few tentative remarks concerning striking parallels between oral epic and Hinojosa's *Klail City* are in order. Those parallels pertain for example to the structuring of the story line. As was noted, Hinojosa's narrative strategy impedes linear development of plot or chronology. It is curious that this is also a prominent feature of the oral epic of antiquity. Ong has pointed to how oral memory is a decisive factor in preventing linearity of plot:

> One of the places where oral mnemonic structures and procedures manifest themselves most spectacularly is in their effect on narrative plot, which in oral culture is not quite what we take plot to be. . . . In fact, an oral culture has no experience of a lengthy epic-size or novel-size climactic linear plot. It cannot organize even shorter narrative in the studious, relentless climactic way that readers of literature for the past 200 years have learned more and more to expect — and, in recent decades, self-consciously to depreciate. . . . You do not find climactic linear plots ready-formed in people's lives. . . .[16]

Ong furthermore observes: "Homer (unconsciously?) organizes the *Iliad* in a geometric pattern like boxes within boxes" (p. 195). Oral poets do not work in a linear fashion due to reliance on memory which does not function in a linear fashion; the direction of a narrative is steered by memory and by associative process. Although we can only speculate as to the motivating forces underlying any narrative, Hinojosa undeniably shares with oral bards the fact of narration taking its own organic course. Explicit reflection upon that seemingly organic process, however, would appear to be a mark of print cultures.

> Estas dos partes . . . *Notas de Klail City y sus alrededores, II*, se incluyen aquí porque salieron como el sarampión: primero calentura, luego comezón seguida por la erupción y no porque el que escribe ya había previsto que aquí cupiesen. . . . Uno desconoce de dónde ha de saltar el conejo diablo de la escritura y tampoco sabe cuándo va a salir. (p. 67)

The absence of a sustained ascending and climactic action has various other implications for narrative structure. For example, there can be no real beginning, middle or end. Hinojosa's *Klail City* is a prime example. We begin in *medias res* with "¡No, no, no y no! No anden con fregaderas." Don Salvador Tamez is angrily arranging the shotgun wedding between his son and Jovita de Anda. Correspondingly, *Klail City* ends without coming to any conclusion. It simply leaves off. A logic other than that of chronological sequence serves to link narrative segments.

Along the same lines, the very concept of creativity in operation within oral poetics differs considerably from that within print culture. Verbal creativity within orality occurs within a set of structuring elements or conventions. These conventions are communally held and recognizable. Print narrative is bound only to whatever conventions it chooses. By thematicizing oral genres, Hinojosa straddles both oral and written cultures.

Concluding Remarks

There is a paradox in Hinojosa's rendering of oral culture in print form. In truth, oral culture ceases to be oral if it is written. The physical human breath of words becomes inanimate print on paper. Words in print cease to exist as a participatory activity in a community. Printed words isolate: people read to themselves; each person reads alone and may or may not share in the culture of those words. Books can be shut, magazines — and all manner of words in print — can be thrown out. And so the fact of their being materialized in print can make them immaterial, inflationary, expendable. Words in oral cultures, however, cannot be put aside or thrown away. Spoken words are always in the context of an existential situation. Human context gives those words their power and makes them material. Written words are always "out of context," separate from the context of the spoken lifeworld.

Hinojosa's *Klail City* narrative cannot be equated with the living world of the Rio Grande Valley. The written representation of that world through forms and techniques inherent to orally based thought and expression make it a hybrid form of oral/written narrative within Chicano literature. It is a vision of community from the oral roots up, not from authorial omniscience down, nor through the eyes of a supposedly "representative" character. Hinojosa truly portrays a community from the inside out in all its naturalness, without the idealization or posturing that mark various works of Chicano literature. In his selection of that particular world, he validates the experience and existence of commmunity and communal oral customs. Hinojosa's narrative perspective and his expressed authorial concern with remembrance, recovery and identity are features common to various Chicano writers who came into their own at the time of the Chicano Movement and the Civil Rights Movement. Recollection and preservation have remained matters of vital concern for many writers even into the 80s.

The phenomenon of Chicanos "breaking into print" is a recent development. Traditionally, from its ancient roots, the culture has been an oral one. Even today the preponderance of poetic expression among Chicanos is oral and sung. That presence makes itself felt in ways in which orality can inform written works. Literary historians, however, have failed to deal with either the strong presence of non-print forms of verbal creativity or with their relationship to literature in print. Critics of Chicano literature strongly reflect that partiality toward the printed word, as well as a corresponding disregard for the creative use of language in oral forms. That disregard might well explain both the dearth of critical writings on *Klail City y sus alrededores* and the omission of oral culture as a consideration by those who have written on this novel.

It cannot surprise us to find that some works of Chicano literature have attracted much more attention than others. Particular types of literary artifice are attractive to established critical schools. A critic's attraction to one work over another — and the nature of his or her treatment of a work — depend upon categories of perception. Most critics' categories are acquired in academic departments of literature, which have traditionally excluded non-print poetic expression from consideration. Critics — including Chicano critics — have internalized that bias. The printed word, after all, is the one which carries authority and sets the standard in centers of political and economic power. Cultural forms more closely associated with human memory and performance are overlooked entirely or considered inconsequential. Print-bound scholars are even prone to view forms of oral culture as quaint, rustic or provincial, generally viewing Mexicano cultural practices as manifestations of a failure to become literate or educated. Oral cultural forms function according to fundamentally different paradigms and premises than works of print culture. In the strongly oral culture found among broad segments of our Chicano population, the word has an entirely different weight, shape, value and function than do words in print, and those values are not entirely lost when oral forms are transposed onto the printed page.

The fundamental assumptions of most critical methodologies are predicated on print culture. Consequently, oral forms, or print forms strongly influenced by oral culture, do not fit upon the procrustean beds of most established schools of literary criticism. Print-bound schools of criticism which , for example, insist upon the autonomy of the individual literary work or upon "autonomous discourse" are quick to eliminate oral poetic forms from consideration, for they are, by definition, not autonomous, but integrated within a life context. Rigorous insistence on the autonomy of literary works furthermore erases the relationship between printed texts and elements from the non-print world, including oral culture. Walter Ong describes some of the new light that an understanding of orality can shed upon various critical methodologies whose exclusive concern with print breeds distortive tendentiousness.[17]

Hinojosa's novel tells us a great deal about the intersection of print culture with oral-aural modes of verbalization. Without reference to those modes his characters and situations might be interpreted as a matter of local color. The categories we bring to literary criticism can potentially illuminate or obscure the artistry of a work. Traditional oral forms and the emerging Chicano literature constitute two coordinates in the complex system of Chicano culture. If we are to address the vital tension between those realms, an increased consciousness of the distinct properties of oral cultural forms is an imperative. Our critical categories must reflect the changing relationship between orality and literacy, and the various ways in which these two realms transform each other as they intersect, merge, and clash.

[1] Rolando Hinojosa, *Klail City und Umgebung*, trans. and epilogue by Yolanda Julia Broyles (Berlin, GDR: Volk & Welt, 1980).

[2] Rolando Hinojosa, *Klail City und Umgebung*, trans. and epilogue by Yolanda Julia Broyles (Frankfurt, FRG: Suhrkamp Verlag, 1981).

[3] Rolando Hinojosa, *Generaciones y semblanzas*, trans. by Rosaura Sánchez (Berkeley: Editorial Justa Publications, 1977). All quotations are from this edition. The original edition was *Klail City y sus alrededores* (Habana: Casa de las Américas, 1976).

[4] For a listing of reviews and essays see Ernestina Eger, *A Bibliography of Criticism of Contemporary Chicano Literature,* Chicano Studies Library Publications of the University of California (Berkeley: University of California Press, 1982), pp. 130-133. The most noteworthy article written on *Klail City* is Donald A. Randolph's "La imprecisión estética en *Klail City y sus alrededores,*" *Revista Chicano-Riqueña* 9/4 (Fall 1981), pp. 52-65.

[5] Fernán Pérez de Guzmán, *Generaciones y semblanzas,* (Buenos Aires: Espasa-Calpe, 1947), pp. 9-10.

[6] Hinojosa, *Generaciones;* this and all subsequent quotations from the preface quoted in this section are on p. 1.

[7] Walter J. Ong, *Orality and Literacy: The Technologizing of the Word* (New York: Methuen, 1982), p. 69.

[8] Américo Paredes, "With His Pistol in his Hand" (Austin: University of Texas Press, 1958) addresses the relationship between the social conflict born of foreign domination and the *corrido.* The response to assimilationist behavior through joking is treated by José Limón, "Agringado Joking," *New Scholar,* 6 (1977) pp. 33-50.

[9] Nicolás Kanellos, "Testimony Given at the American Writers Congress," *Revista Chicano-Riqueña,* 9, No. 4 (Fall 1981), pp. 1-3.

[10] Hinojosa, *Generaciones,* p. 17.

[11] Hinojosa, *Generaciones;* all quotations of Jehú Malacara are on pp. 136-137.

[12] Narratologists have posited various features considered to be constitutive of most narrative works. Most of those concepts, however, do not appear applicable to *Klail City.* The common story/discourse dichotomy is blurred in *Klail City,* where story (what is said, content) and discourse (the means of expression) are largely inextricable. The oral genres portrayed are charged with a communal meaning independent of each realization. Each oral performance creates meaning to some extent independently of literal action (story). Narratologists also posit a hierarchy of narrative events, in which some are more important than others. Those allegedly more important events are known as kernels or *motif associé,* the less important ones as satellites or *motif libre.* This distinction also hardly seems applicable to *Klail City* whose events hardly fall into hierarchical order. For a discussion of these concepts

and their application in narrative theory, see Seymour Chatham, *Story and Discourse: Narrative Structure in Fiction and Film* (Ithaca: Cornell University Press, 1980).

[13]This development is described in various books, including Erich Kahler's *The Inward Turn of Narrative,* trans. by Richard and Clara Winston (Princeton, N.J.: Princeton University Press, 1973).

[14]That is not to imply that all Chicanos participate in that culture. *Klail City* includes reference to what are called "desposeídos" (assimilated Mexicans) who do not speak Spanish. These "desposeídos" stand in contrast to those children who have maintained their cultural identity: "Estos, 'los desposeídos'. . . . hablaban mejor inglés que uno pero ni siquiera sabían defenderse, (e.g. en las aulas o en el recreo. Nosotros . . . como sabíamos quienes éramos y qué éramos), exigíamos footballs tan buenos como las que les daban a la bolillada" (p. 67).

[15]Interview of Rolando Hinojosa by Francisco Lomelí, May 11, 1981, (TS), p. 15.

[16]Walter Ong, *Orality and Literacy,* p. 141-43.

[17]Walter Ong, *Orality and Literacy,* Chapter 7.

Héctor Calderón
Yale University

On the Uses of Chronicle, Biography and Sketch in
Rolando Hinojosa's *Generaciones y semblanzas*

Although Rolando Hinojosa's shared sensibility with Julio ✓
Torri, the Mexican *costumbrista* writer of *estampas* or sketches,
has been noted by Raymund Paredes (100) and Sabine Ulibarrí
and Dick Gerdes (158), nothing has been written verifying
Hinojosa's debt to an important work of Spanish historiography
of the period of transition from the Medieval Age to the Renaissance. In his own unique way, Hinojosa continues in the tradition of Latin American *costumbrismo;* however, his works
should be read along with recent Latin American books imagi-
natively conceived around the narrative elements of a chronicle
of which the most popular is *Cien años de soledad.* Hinojosa's
insistence on genealogies, factual data and recent historical
events leads the reader to interpret his fictions against the background of the history of the Río Grande Valley. It can be said that
his fragmentary tales of Belken County form a mosaic in which
the reader fits each piece or sketch within a linear narrative, and
only by stepping back, after reading his published works and
seeing the larger picture, can we appreciate the sum total of his
books as a vast "cronicón del condado de Belken." These are the
words chosen by the writers Jehú Malacara in *Generaciones y
semblanzas* (169) and P. Galindo in *Mi querido Rafa* (8) to
describe their work. But more importantly, Hinojosa has
adopted a title for his work that refers directly to Fernán Pérez de
Guzmán's *Generaciones y semblanzas* written c. 1450. The
purpose of this essay is not so much to compare the Chicano
version with its Spanish predecessor but to understand what use
Hinojosa makes of the tradition of the chronicle narrated as a
series of biographical sketches.

I

Through personal eye-witness, *memorial,* and written documents, *registro,* Guzmán derives his characters and events from

the recent history of Spanish kingdoms prior to the unification of the peninsula under the Catholic Kings. Guzmán chronicles a world of seignorial estates and powerful patriarchal families in which the *caballería* is still important, but it is also a world in transition contrasting a prior warrior ethic with a more gentlemanly or aristocratic view of manhood based on a virtuous life. A primitive conception of character and personality allows Guzmán to write his history as a series of *semblanzas* or biographical sketches. Classical biography, of which Guzmán was well aware, had reached a similar stage of development. For example, Plutarch in his *Lives* aimed at representing character, virtues and vices not through glorious deeds, but through trivial actions. Just as a portrait painter, explained Plutarch, attemped to show likeness (*semblanza* could be a substitute) through features, physiognomy (*semblante* is also useful), he would represent each individual life through the signs of the psyche (225). As in Plutarch's accounts of famous men, in Guzmán's narrative, the flow of events is secondary to more imaginative, rhetorical and didactic demands. In each sketch he establishes a lineage, describes physical characteristics disclosing temperaments and moral qualities, "semblantes e costumbres, faciones e condiciones" (4). In all cases men's actions were to be judged by the cardinal virtues of prudence, temperance, fortitude and justice.

In terms of the history of narrative forms, Guzmán's sketches could be empirical forerunners and complements to later realistic fiction (the novel, for example) in which an imagined character and his or her world are actualized so as to convey to the reader a sense of reality. In sharp distinction with Medieval romance, Guzmán demonstrates a mimetic impulse when he warns against chroniclers "de poca vergüenza e mas les plaze relatar cosas estrañas e maravillosas que verdaderas e ciertas" (1). Yet any modern reader would be hardpressed to find novelistic characters in the work of Guzmán simply because he writes in a time prior to the development of a conceptual apparatus, most notably Aristotle's *Poetics*, that gave rise to the novel. Guzmán's sketches are basically anecdotal, describing incidents without elaborating a plot of sufficient length to allow a change in character based on what is probable, logical or necessary. In his sketches, the reader will not be rewarded with characters of any depth who reach a self-awareness normally guaranteed by a later, more conceptualized, faculty psychology.

The limits of the biographical sketch as a narrative form can be understood through the analogy with the visual arts. Just as a portrait painter can isolate a bidimensional moment for the viewer's attention, the sketch can interrupt the flow of past-present-future and present a static moment in which only the most prominent or objective and often superficial characteristics, features of a character or a group stand out. The legacy of the biographical sketch can lead to the unimaginative form of the *cuadro de costumbres* of Latin American fiction, a form vehemently rejected by contemporary writers.

II

Hinojosa's *Generaciones y semblanzas* is similar in form and content to its Spanish ancestor, and in this sense the work participates within the tradition of *costumbrismo*. The Board of Jurors who gave the book the Casa de las Américas prize for Novel in 1976 were correct in pointing out its testimonial or documentary value and Hinojosa's descriptive vigor and use of dialectical and colloquial speech patterns. And yet, this loosely-jointed book departs from the traditional presentation of the sketch pattern of *semblanzas*. The demands placed upon the reader's participatory activities are evident in the lack of an omniscient narrator to guide the reader's understanding through the narrative fragments paratactically conceived without any causal links among them. The reader is overwhelmed by the sheer inventiveness of Hinojosa: multiple narrators who collaborate as chroniclers (Rafa Buenrostro, Jehú Malacara, P. Galindo) of Belken County; a wide variety of settings; narrative presentation through monologues, dialogues, written documents, letters and radio announcements. Time frames of past and present are juxtaposed in dizzying fashion not just within a single text, but also between books. For example, the story of the feud between the Buenrostros and the Leguizamóns narrated in the first sections of *Generaciones y semblanzas* published in 1977 reaches a resolution in the testimonies contained within *Rites and Witnesses* (67-68, 76, 86-89) published in 1982. Although the sketches are not presented in a straightforward, linear chronicle, the reader attains a better perspective with each book. In a most innovative way, the chronicle of Belken County and Klail City is narrated and relived from an indeterminate present which should be interpreted as that place of fiction where the writer's imagination meets the reader.

The first section of Hinojosa's tripartite *Generaciones y semblanzas* is the one inspired by Guzmán's chronicle and the only part of his book that Hinojosa intended to be titled after its predecessor.[1] Each part of the book has its own independent figurative framework divided into ten narrative segments. "Generaciones y semblanzas"/Generations and Sketches" establishes a temporal progression for the book with the death of don Jesús Buenrostro. "Notas de Klail City y sus alredededores, II"/"Notes from Klail City and Its Environs, II" maps out a spatial projection for the residents of Klail City from Mexico through the states of the West and the Midwest such as Colorado, Indiana and Michigan. "Brechas nuevas y viejas"/"Trails Old and New" brings to completion unresolved narrative plots from the two previous sections. However different each section may be, they are given a sense of order in time and space through the intratextual references to the death of don Jesús Buenrostro.

The initial section establishes a genealogy, an historical legitimacy within the Río Grande Valley for the characters, narrators and writers Rafa Buenrostro and Jehú Malacara (who in a later book turn out to be cousins). While the reader is being led astray by the biographical sketches of the forceful don Salvador Tamez, the drunk Echevarría, the Texas Ranger Choche Markham, the Sheriff Big Foot Parkinson, in a subtle way Hinojosa is describing a world similar to that of Guzman's Spain.

After reading the chronicle of Belken County through the latest book, it is understood that the world of the Rio Grande Valley is in transition, from an older generation born in the nineteenth century and still very much attached to Hispanic and Mexican values, to the adolescent world of Rafa and Jehú set in the 1940's. For the unabashedly masculine world of the powerful Mexican ranching families — the Buenrostros, Leguizamóns, Vilches, Campoys and Farías — the Spanish terms "claros varones" and "hombres rectos y cabales," complete men as well as real gentlemen, still mean more than any American ideology of individualism and personal identity. When Hinojosa sets the action of this initial section in this century, he is emphasizing the persistence of a rural way of life of *rancheros* still very much tied to the soil. Hinojosa fuses both history and culture when he describes in a few sentences the circumstances surrounding the death of the patriarch of the Buenrostro clan. When don Jesús is killed out on the lands of his Carmen Ranch, his brother don Julián lays the body across his horse and walks to his brother's house and sets him at the foot of a huge pecan tree (21); later, don Julián rides his horse across the border into Mexico in search of his brother's murderers (23).

The death of don Jesús functions as a leitmotif and is recalled by different characters in all three sections of the book. The image of the fallen hero produces a nostalgia for a better Mexican past within the changing world of Belken County. This is certainly the case with the oldtimers who recall him: Esteban Echevarría in a bar among his friends; Leocadio Gavira in his travels through the Midwest with migrant workers; and don Marcial de Anda sitting on his park bench while talking to Rafa. But this leitmotif has a greater rhetorical effectiveness because through it Hinojosa takes up a theme common to the tradition of biography for which Pérez de Guzmán has served as a model. The attitude of this biographer toward his characters was that of a moralist: the life of an important historical personage emphasized posthumous fame as an ethical force within society.[2] In his prologue, he distinguishes between those men who were desirous of fame and, therefore, might be deceitful and those men who through their deeds deserved it. Guzmán's openly-stated aims were to preserve in letters the fame and glory of his departed countrymen, to record heroic deeds as well as to depict virtue and vice with utility and profit for the reader.

Although don Jesús appears only very briefly in the second part of the book speaking one line (77), the reader is persuaded to accept him as a man of great stature. There are obvious symbolic interpretations that should be derived from his name. The Buenrostro name is a reference to the tradition of the biographical sketch; he has a good countenance, *semblante,* and, therefore, according to a semiotics of the body and the rules of portraiture his face discloses good moral qualities. Like Christ he dies in spring and his life will be a force and a standard to judge good men. His name also reminds us of García Márquez' José Arcadio Buendía. Both men are titular heads of a lineage of men (although Hinojosa proceeds by understatement and García Márquez by hyperbole and satire); both men are symbolically laid to rest by a tree near their home. Moreover, the fame that is accorded to don Jesús is not sought after; it is freely given by his people who remember him with the epithets, "don Jesús Buenrostro, el quieto, hombre recto y cabal."

The clearly-sketched outline of this absent and silent figure assumes an overwhelming symbolic presence as a point of comparison with other male characters. Given the moral qualities of don Jesús, two other men stand out in a positive light. Don Manuel Guzmán, the policeman of the Chicano barrio of Klail City, goes about his work quietly with a good heart, *buen corazón,* for his friends and the downtrodden. This quality is clearly evident in his compassion for Julie, the black prostitute, who shot her lover in self-defense and for don Aureliano Mora who destroyed a plaque honoring war veterans as protest for the murder of his son, a veteran, at the hands of a Sheriff's deputy. Tom Purdy, the northern school teacher, is remembered fondly by P. Galindo for his kindness. Without talking to federal, state and local authorities nor the press, without hesitation, Purdy and his wife quietly aided Chicano migrant workers who, because they were people, deserved to be treated as such.

Hinojosa's poetic liberties with the Buenrostro name can yield latent political interpretations. In the third section, in a poignant scene with don Manual Guzmán, don Aureliano Mora compares the historical situation of Mexicans and Chicanos within Texas to Greek slaves living under the Roman Empire. The first section, therefore, should be reread intratextually as a rendering of parallel lives, characters, comparing and contrasting two social groups in opposition. This is, incidentally, a pattern followed by the Greek Plutarch who, like Hinojosa, wrote in his native language while living under Roman rule. Against the unassuming figure of don Jesús, Hinojosa portrays two Anglo figures of authority. The loud oratory of the comical Sheriff Parkinson does not deceive Chicanos. Although he attempts to use Spanish, he does so solely to gain people's favor for his own political aspirations. Esteban Echevarría describes the Texas Ranger Choche (George) Markham as cowardly, opportunistic and deceitful. He too presents himself as a friend of *la raza* using Spanish to win their friendship. However, this does not hide his complicitous relationship with the Anglo ranchers, the Klails, Blanchards and Cookes, and the Leguizamóns who paid Mexican nationals to kill don Jesús (see *Rites and Witnesses,* 88). Through the portraits of don Jesús, Hinojosa rewrites the past in terms of the political maneuvering, racism and violence that went on in the border area from the turn of the century through later decades when don Jesús was murdered. To understand the demystification of the famous Rangers (notorious from the Chicanos' perspective), the reader should compare the Spanish voices in *Generaciones y semblanzas* with the English voices in *Rites and Witnesses.* John F. Good testifies describing the Rangers' actions: "The Rangers raised hell . . . and they murdered people . . . that's the word all right, and there's nothing else to call it" (86). Perhaps the most damaging testimony is supplied by Markham himself when he admits to having killed don Aureliano's son (76).

III

The oppositional nature of Hinojosa's discourse offers important insights into the form of his fictions. The biographical sketch pattern in the tradition of classical biography and Spanish chronicle allows Hinojosa to portray characters through anecdote, a single incident or a single series of episodes without the need for the internal development of a protagonist's mind. Hinojosa has chosen this form because his characters are already formed by a Mexican, Spanish-speaking culture.[3]

The majority of Chicano narratives are structured according to the rhetoric of a *bildungsroman* with a story of a male character or hero highlighting the problems of identity, between, on the one hand, being an American, and, on the other, searching for one's Chicano identity or one's Indian, Mexican or Hispanic roots. In the more technical aspects of this narrative emplotment, the reader recognizes a central protagonist with subordinate or secondary characters, all in some way or another contributing to a final resolution. In Hinojosa's fiction, the reader is confounded by the lack of an individual character that demands our attention. The chroniclers Rafa and Galindo do not really qualify. Although Jehú Malacara's sections are episodic and structured in the autobiographical form of a picaresque narrative, in Hinojosa's works to date no thoughts are analyzed, no character achieves a moment of illumination or inward self-awareness.

Hinojosa's fictional world seems untouched by the Chicano movement because, given the historical conditions in Texas, his characters already know who they are. Although the writers Rafa and Jehú have been through the Armed Forces, although they have attended the University of Texas at Austin, although they function in English in an Anglo world, they have also attended Spanish schools, they speak and write Spanish, they are still Mexicans or Chicanos. In Junior High, Jehú refers to the assimilated, English-speaking Chicanos of the South Ward of Klail City as the dispossessed because they did not come from a barrio with a Spanish name, because they were probably ashamed to speak Spanish, because they did not know how to stand up for themselves against the Anglo students and teachers. Judging from his most outspoken character, Hinojosa through the first books of his *cronicón* wants to stress the collective character, the many lives, of a social group formed in opposition to dominance and without much superstructural modification by American ideology.

[1]Hinojosa submitted his three-part manuscript to Casa de las Américas without a complete title. The Board of Jurors gave it the provisional title of *Klail City y sus alrededores*. Justa Publications published the work with the title of the first section.

[2]For the function of fame in Guzmán's *Generaciones y semblanzas,* see Lida de Malkiel's brief comments (269-74).

[3]There is a gap that needs to be filled describing the generation prior to Rafa and Jehú. This will soon be remedied by the publication of the long-awaited *Claros varones de Belken* whose title was inspired by another Spanish chronicle, Fernando del Pulgar's *Claros varones de Castilla*.

Works Cited

Hinojosa, Rolando. *Generaciones y semblanzas*. Berkeley, Calif.: Editorial Justa Publications, Inc., 1977.

———. *Mi querido Rafa*. Houston, Texas: Arte Público Press, 1981.

———. *Rites and Witnesses: A Comedy*. Houston, Texas: Arte Público Press, 1982.

Lida de Malkiel, María Rosa. *La idea de la fama en la edad media castellana*. México: Fondo de Cultura Económica, 1952.

Paredes, Raymund A. "The Evolution of Chicano Literature." *MELUS* 5/2 (1978):71-110.

Pérez de Guzmán, Fernán. *Generaciones y semblanzas*. Ed. Robert Brian Tate. London: Tamesis Books Limited, 1965.

Plutarch. *The Parallel Lives*. Trans. Bernadotte Perrin. 11 vols. Loeb Classical Library Series. New York: G. P. Putnam's Sons, 1928. Vol. 7.

Pulgar, Fernando del. *Claros varones de Castilla*. Ed. Robert Brian Tate. Oxford: Clarendon Press, 1971.

Ulibarrí, Sabine and Dick Gerdes. "Mexican Literature and Chicano Literature: A Comparison." In *Ibero-American Letters in a Comparative Perspective.* Ed. Wolodymyr T. Zyla and Wendell M. Aycock. Proceedings of the Comparative Literature Symposium, Vol. 10. 26-28 Jan. 1978. Lubbock, Texas: Texas Tech Press, 1978, 149-67.

Ramón Saldívar
University of Texas at Austin

Korean Love Songs:
A Border Ballad and its Heroes

Américo Paredes has argued in his now classic study of the *corridos* dealing with the figure of Gregorio Cortez that, before Border balladry entered its decadent period in the 1930s, it was working toward a single type: "toward one form, the *corrido*; toward one theme, border conflict; toward one concept of the hero, the man fighting for his right with his pistol in his hand".[1] The old ballad subjects dealing primarily with everyday life lose their interest and the hero becomes the peaceful man who defends his right. "Gregorio Cortez" thus establishes a pattern: "The hero is always the peaceful man, finally goaded into violence by the *rinches* and rising in his wrath to kill great numbers of his enemy. His defeat is assured; at the best he can escape across the border, and often he is killed or captured. But whatever his fate, he has stood up for his rights" (Paredes, p. 149). The heroic type of the *corrido* is thus created in opposition to Anglo-American characters and institutions, which serve as "reacting agents" (Paredes, p. 247) against which individual and cultural identity may be forged. Ten years before the Mexican Revolution, the interracial and class struggles which will become the focus of literary and everyday reality of South Texas are evident "already in full vigor in *El Corrido de Gregorio Cortez*" (Paredes, p. 247).

I wish to examine briefly in this essay the transformation of the complex of issues raised by border *corridos,* such as *"Gregorio Cortez,"* in Rolando Hinojosa's narrative poem, *Korean Love Songs: From Klail City Death Trip.*[2] The events of Hinojosa's poem, I will argue, form a roughly analogous formal and thematic parallel with early twentieth-century *corridos*. But in the intervening years between the creation of "Gregorio Cortez" and *Korean Love Songs* historical circumstances have changed, so that while racial and class struggle continue to be the concerns of the sensitive artist, the formulation, confrontation, and attempted reconciliation of that struggle by the poetic hero have changed dramatically.

Not the least of the factors involved in our understanding of the difference between Mexican American narrative verse of the early twentieth century and that of late-century are the changing notions of literary modernism with its attendant sense of so-called high culture, and of folk art, with its different sense of cultural valuation. I think that a brief consideration of these issues will help us to understand why in his contemporary manifestation in Hinojosa's long narrative poem the mid-century Mexican American ballad hero remains the analogue of the hero of the earlier *corrido* in vastly redressed form. I suggest that, like *El Corrido de Gregorio Cortez,* Hinojosa's *Korean Love Songs* has as its underlying impulse — albeit in symbolic and unconscious form — some of our deepest fantasies about the nature of social life, both as we live it and as we would like to have it be. The difference is that in the earlier song this impulse can be expressed directly and literally, whereas in the later song the impulse can be expressed only indirectly and figuratively.

I begin my discussion at a theoretical remove by turning first, and briefly, to the theory of culture worked out by the Frankfurt School in the work of Adorno, Horkheimer, and Marcuse. Their work provides an important working methodology for the close analysis of the literary products of culture in the contemporary American scene. As Fredric Jameson points out in an essay entitled "Reification and Utopia in Mass Culture," the work of the Frankfurt School can be characterized "as the extension and application of Marxist theories of commodity reification to the works of mass culture."[3] When addressed from this perspective, the function of art, its unique and distinct "ends" or value, must be understood in terms of its *use function,* its "instrumentality."

Under capitalism, older forms of human activity, including aesthetic ones, are instrumentally reorganized and analytically fragmented in order to be reconstructed according to models of efficiency and profitability. In traditional activity, artistic or otherwise, as Jameson suggests, "the value of the activity is immanent to it, and qualitatively distinct from other ends or values articulated in other forms of human work or play" (pp. 130-1). It is only with the commodification of labor power that all forms of human work can be "separated out from their unique qualitative differentiation as distinct types of activity" (p. 131). Once this separating out of the differentiating aspects of human work has occurred, all work can be reclassified and hence reunderstood in terms not of its immanent value but of its instrumentality.

In a world where everything, including labor power, has become a commodity, the instrumentality, the ends of cultural productions, come to create the conditions for their own consumption. The commodity produced by human labor "no longer has any qualitative value in itself, but only insofar as it can be 'used' " (Jameson, p. 131). The objects of the commodity world of capitalism, as Jameson goes on to suggest, "shed their independent 'being' and intrinsic qualities and come to be so many instruments of commodity satisfaction" (p. 131). Everything in consumer society thus takes on an aesthetic dimension, to the extent that its consumption becomes literally or figuratively a sensual experience.

Although a fuller discussion of the applicability of the theories of the Frankfurt School to contemporary conditions would have to qualify and reformulate some of that group's conclusions, for the present discussion this schematic survey of their notion of cultural theory provides a convenient beginning point. It helps us to specify, at the very least, some of the basic differences between popular folk art, and in particular the folk art of the past, and the products of contemporary high art or mass culture. As Professor Paredes has so definitively established, for example, it is the case that the border ballads, the *corridos,* of the early twentieth century reflected and depended on for their production a different social reality than that which produces mainstream "high" or "popular" art in the late twentieth century. And while it may still be the case that contemporary Mexican American literature is the "organic" expression of a distinct community, a unified social group with its own cultural specificity not yet totally compromised by the effects of mass market economy, the historical effect of late capitalism to dissolve and fragment organic communities into isolated and atomized agglomerations of private individuals is too well known to be ignored. The individualized voice of the unique artistic sensibility represented among Chicanos by Richard Rodriguez is one example of this disruption of the organic Mexican American community. It thus behooves us to understand the conditions under which the ideological force of the early twentieth century border ballad of the peaceful man struggling for social justice "with his pistol in his hand" has been preserved, even if in altered form, in late twentieth century Mexican American narrative verse.

The typical *corrido* situation posits, as we have seen, a common, peaceful, working man put into an uncommon situation by the power of cultural and historical forces beyond his control. The *corrido* hero is forced to give up his natural way of life by his attempts to defend his home, his family, his very community. In the process of his attempt to win social justice, his concern for his own personal life and his own solitary fate must be put aside for the good of the collective life of his social group. Composed for a predominantly rural folk and focused on a specific geographical locale, the unity of the *corrido* is culturally, temporally, and spatially specific; the *corrido* makes no effort to be "literary" or "universal." Its point of view is cultural rather than national (Paredes, pp. 183-4). And since its principal aim is narrative, the *corrido* concentrates on the actions of the hero: "Though it avoids for the most part comments from the narrator and all unnecessary detail, the *corrido* gives a fairly complete account of the facts. . . . (T)he narrative style is swift and compact; it is composed into scenes; there is a liberal amount of dialogue" (Paredes, p. 188). In style and form, the *corrido* is thus the product of the collective imagination of a community whose environment was border conflict.

Only against the background of the later bifurcation of time and plot in Chicano narrative fiction can we get a sense of the immanent unity of the *corrido's* forms and themes. The hero's individual life-sequences have not yet become totally distinct from those of his community; the private sphere of interior consciousness has not yet become the concern of the balladeer; the private quality of life has not yet coalesced into a central, independent identity that is distinct from the identity of the community. Life is one and it is "historicized" to the extent that all existential factors, are not merely aspects of a personal life but are a common affair, as M. M. Bakhtin has argued concerning the nature of folk art in general.[4] On the Texas-Mexican border, the *corrido* drew its vitality from the social and collective status of the community, from the fact that the relationship between balladeer and audience, that is to say between aesthetic producer and consumer, was still that of "pre-capitalist" modes of aesthetic production, "a social institution and a concrete social and interpersonal relationship with its own validation and specificity" (Jameson, p. 136).

Rolando Hinojosa's *Korean Love Songs* (1978) tells the *corrido* story of border conflict and social justice in the symbolically displaced form of the long narrative poem and the ideologically different context of the Korean War. The hero in this case, however, is not an idyllic figure of communal solidarity like Gregorio Cortez, but rather the orphaned and eccentric Rafa Buenrostro. The issue is not the conflict inherent in a cultural and political border but a real war precipitated from an abstract conflict between world powers and their surrogates. And yet, what remains constant, and links Hinojosa's poem with the grand tradition of the border *corrido,* is the poem's thematization of cultural integrity, communal identity, and social justice. As paradoxical as this claim may seem, given that the entire action of *Korean Love Songs* is set in Japan and Korea, it can be shown, I think, that Hinojosa's poem, like the *corridos* that form its generic models, is about South Texas and Mexican American life in a moment of crucial self-definition.

Unlike the situation of contemporary "high" art, in which

capitalism has so dissolved the fabric of all cohesive social groups that an authentic aesthetic production having its source in group life is practically impossible, *Korean Love Songs* is an example of Mexican American art struggling to maintain its existence as an expression of an organic social life. In Hinojosa's poem we are offered a moment in this struggle to understand and retain a genuine cultural and historical class consciousness within the ever encroaching insistence of late capitalist social life. But unlike its own folkloric base, the early *corrido,* Hinojosa's poem must enact its representation of this struggle not from the outside, as one between Anglo-American cultural and political institutions and Mexican American ones, but from within, as the central Chicano characters become representatives of American cultural and political power as embodied in its armed forces. I thus argue that Hinojosa's *Korean Love Songs* represents the tradition of folk art even while it differs greatly from it, just as it draws from the tradition of literary modernism even while it sets its own separate course. To see this set of issues at work let us turn to a close reading of the poem.

In another place I have maintained that in Hinojosa's novels narrative time is fluid and that characters in the present seem to co-exist temporally with characters from the past.[5] Because of this temporal instability, Hinojosa's novels tend to be less about individual subjects and unique personalities than about the collective social life of the Mexican American community of the Lower Rio Grande Valley of Texas. The collective social life becomes a "character" in its own right, a kind of disembodied consciousness that attains almost heroic proportions. In *Korean Love Songs* this pattern continues and serves as perhaps the single most important difference between this work's narrative thrust and that of the traditional *corrido.* Whereas in a song like "Gregorio Cortez" the actions of the hero serve at least initially as the organizing focus of the story, in Hinojosa's *Korean Love Songs* there is no "hero" in the traditional sense. The action represented in the poem must be read not as the story of "individuals," nor as the chronicle of a generation and its destiny, but as the dispersed history of impersonal forces. The central narrative of the work is not Rafa Buenrostro's but is immediately deflected on the opening pages of the text to "the four of us", (*KLS*, p. 5), that is, David "Sonny" Ruiz, José Vielma, Rosalío "Charlie" Villalón, and Rafa Buenrostro. Jacob Mosqueda and Cayo Díaz Balderas later join this initial group. As the narrative proceeds, the personal identity of this cluster of characters is superseded first by the impersonal anonymity of the 219th Field Artillery Battalion in which they serve, then by the institutional identity provided by the U. S. Eighth Army, and finally by the masking quality of the Korean and Japanese cultures within which these displaced Chicanos find themselves.

Even Rafa Buenrostro, who as the narrator of the poem commands our attention as a singular voice, cannot be considered as the "hero" or protagonist of the story in any traditional sense. He is not the central actor precipitating the outcome of the historical action, but a peripheral mediator, serving as a link between his own Mexican American culture, the Anglo-American institutions represented starkly by the demands of army life, and the ritualized Japanese way of life. In one significant scene Rafa must swear before an army board of inquiry that Sonny Ruiz, whom he knows to be alive and well and living in Japan, is dead. Rafa, the literal and symbolic orphan of the story ("two orphans, she and I," Rafa later says in reference to his friend Hanako Kokada and himself (p. 48), serves the odd function of giving Sonny Ruiz a new Japanese life by taking away his former Mexican American one.

Having been wounded by a rocket blast that has killed his friend Joey Vielma, Rafa is given an "R & R Medical leave" in Japan after his release from an army hospital. He has arranged to meet Sonny, who has gone AWOL and disappeared into Japanese life, at the Tanaka Tea Gardens in Nagoya, Japan. Because the passage is so important, I quote it at length:

> Many uniforms around us, but again no familiar patch or
> face.

It's eight forty, and the Tanaka Tea Gardens, a mile off,
Is where I'm to meet Sonny Ruiz,
Who these many months
Has been AWOL (and reported missing sometimes, and
         dead at others).
They'll never find him; to begin with,
To Americans he looks Japanese; For another,
No one really gives a damn, one way or another. The
Army,
For all its pretense,
Is not led by divine guidance.

Sonny of the *old,* old 219th and twice wounded, made
         corporal and stopped;
One day he filled out and signed his own
         Missing-In-Action cards.
Just like so much equipment;
He personally turned them over to battery HQ,
Then simply walked away to the docks.

Army efficiency being what it is immediately produced
         a replacement
Who promptly went mad during practice fire,
And that was the end of that.
Not long after, cards started to arrive from Nagoya and
         signed
By Mr. Kazuo Fusaro who, in another life,
Had lived as David Ruiz in Klail City,
And who, in his new life,
Was now a hundred and ten per cent Japanese.

There he is, punctual as death: Business suit, hat,
         arms at his side,
And as I approach, he fills the air with konnichi wahs,
As he bends lower and lower, arms still at his side,
         smiling the while.

> He and I are the only ones left:
>> Charlie Villalón, Joey Vielma, Cayo Díaz
>> And a kid named Balderas
> Have all been erased from the Oriental scene. . . .
>
> Business is fine, and he is marrying later in the fall;
>> a schoolteacher, no less.
> And home?
>
> "*This* is home, Rafe. Why should I go back?"
>> (*KLS*, p. 43)

This passage may be easily misread. On one hand, we have Sonny's apparently complete assimilation into Japanese society. Rafa's words that "To Americans he looks Japanese" are bolstered a few lines later when an American M. P. looks straight at Sonny and his flower bouquet and "grunts" to his friend: "Pipe the gook and them flowers, there./ Damndest place I've ever seen" (*KLS*, p. 45). From the Anglo-American perspective, all non-Anglos look and are alike. Given this uniformity, we might be lulled into believing that the assimilation of a cultural identity is indeed simple. Interestingly enough, this view that filters out the real historical differences between Mexican American and Japanese life and their cultural expressions is also Sonny's, who is "now a hundred and ten per cent Japanese." From Sonny's perspective, the cultural affinity between Japanese and Mexican American life allows for this assimilation and its resulting turn away from an oppressed, self-negating home in South Texas.

And yet on the other hand, Rafa, who will return "to Klail, And home. Home to Texas, our Texas,/ That slice of hell, heaven,/Purgatory and land of our Fathers" (*KLS*, p. 53), uses his narrative material to sharpen our senses of the historical differences between Anglo-Americans and Japanese, Chicanos and Japanese, as well as between Anglos and Chicanos, and to stimulate an apprehension of what happens and what we would have happen when cultures meet. Sonny Ruiz has found the utopian opposite to "That slice of hell, heaven,/Purgatory and land of our Fathers" to which Rafa will return.

A few pages later, before the army Board of Inquiry into Sonny Ruiz's "death," Rafa says:

> The Board of Inquiry wishes to ascertain
> Facts relative to
> The matter of Cpl. David Ruiz's death
> In battle action in the summer of 1951.
> On a Government Issued bible, I swear
> That, to the very best of my knowledge,
> Cpl. Ruiz is dead.
>
>   At parade rest,
> Before the Board,
> I think of old, mad Tina Ruiz, the widow of Ortega,
> Who lost another son, Chano,
> On a sixth of June, a few years back.
> She's Sonny Ruiz's sole beneficiary, and she's worth
>   a howitzer or two;
>
>   And so I lie. . . .
> It comes down to this: we're pieces of equipment
> To be counted and signed for.
>
>   On occasion some of us break down,
> And those parts which can't be salvaged
> Are replaced with other GI parts, that's all.
> (*KLS,* pp. 49-50)

In the face of a de-individualization which is also dehumanizing, Rafa's lie before the board of inquiry is a de-individualization of Sonny Ruiz that paradoxically gives him back an identity of his own, albeit not the one in which he lived his former life in Klail City. Rafa's "lie" before the board of inquiry on behalf of Sonny Ruiz overcomes both one aspect of Sonny's isolated, autonomous subjectivity and the anonymous absorption of that subjectivity by the American army. As Rafa realizes: "I work for the State" (*KLS*, p. 51), and he may acquiesce to its transformation of his own identity into forms it approves of, or he may subvert its de-individualizing intentions by re-inventing a character for his friend. In having become "Just like so much equipment" (*KLS*, p. 43) "to be counted and signed for" (*KLS*, p. 50), Rafa in Korea and Japan begins to feel a sense of the way in which capitalist institutions use human lives in terms of their"instrumentality." He even acquires the words to begin to understand his predicament: as a chaplain reads from the Introductory Rubric to the *Burial of the Dead* ("violent hands upon themselves" (*KLS*, p. 51), Rafa mulls:

. . . (H)e's reading it from a book,
And I suppose anyone of *us*,
Could have done *that*,
Except
For the fact
That we don't belong to the same union;
Our guild furnishes the bodies;
And his, the prayers. Division of labor it's called.
    (*KLS*, p. 51).

The classical marxian analysis shows that the division of labor inside a nation leads to the separation of industrial and commercial from agricultural labor, and then to the separation of town and country and to the conflict of their interests. Its further development leads to the separation of commercial from industrial labor. At the same time, through this division of labor, there develops within the various separated branches of labor, divisions among the individual laborers which now preclude the cooperation of individuals in definite kinds of labor.[6] Out of the unity of laboring men and women, the separation and division of singular and competing individuals is thus created. These same conditions of separation operate at the level of the production of ideas, as expressed in the language of politics, laws, morality, religion, or aesthetics of a people. Separated out into "guilds," Rafa recognizes, individual action is parceled out and reconstituted into efficiently controllable instrumentalities. Some kill while others pray; these distinctive activities define them consequently as one or the other exclusively, a soldier or a priest:

> Our guild furnishes the bodies;
> And his the prayers.

Stating the situation in this manner allows Rafa to understand that to assert himself as an individual he must regain that pre-separatist collective expression which has been the legacy of his people. The police action in Korea thus becomes an analogue of the commodification of labor power and its resultant separating out of the differentiating aspects of human communities which Rafa's homeland must resist — prey to a system in which everyone and everything are "replaceable parts" (*KLS,* p. 50).

These scenes in *Korean Love Songs* are crucial because they seem to project a utopian fantasy about cultural synthesis. Sonny Ruiz is able to find in Japan what he cannot possess at home: "Why should I go back?", he asks. "Why, indeed?" answers Rafa, as he too seems drawn to the fantasy of annihilating the past and starting absolutely anew. This alien world seems rich to them in contrast to the one to which they must return, especially as men like Rafa's company commander Captain "Tex" Bracken and General Walton H. ("a lot of Mexicans live in Texas") Walker "reminded (us) who we were/Thousands of miles from home" (*KLS,* p. 11). Objects of prejudice and exploitation at home, dying in Korea "Creating history by protecting the world from Communism" (*KLS* p. 11), it is no wonder that they are charmed by the allure of Japanese self-sufficiency, integrity, and family solidarity in the face of an occupying American army.

Rafa begins to understand that as little as he knows about the Chinese troops he kills by the "hundreds," so does the army know or care little about him. But he chooses not to turn against his American home. As we already know from the previous novel in the *Klail City Death Trip* series, *Generaciones y semblanzas* (1977), the Texas home to which the Korean War veterans will return is no different from the one to which the World War II veterans returned.[7] It is a place where veterans like Ambrosio Mora, who saw Chano Ortega, the half-brother of Sonny Ruiz, die at Normandy, can be murdered by the local Sheriff's deputy in broad daylight "en frente de la J. C. Penney en el centro de Flora un domingo de palmas" (*GS,* p. 145). We know too from that novel that while the veterans will protest that "ellos también habían ido a la guerra y que bastaba con 'ese pedo de la *discriminación*' " (*GS,* p. 147), the Sheriff's deputy will go free, leaving old Mora only the futile protest gesture of destroying with a crowbar the monument in honor of the local war dead erected by "las damas auxiliares de la American Legion" (*GS,* p. 147). The marker is an empty sign and, like the mass grave with its innumerable neat crosses that Rafa and Joey Vielma once visited to pay their last respects to Charlie Villalón, no one should believe "that the marker is reserved for you" (*KLS,* p. 24).

And yet, at the moment he is wounded, Rafa's thoughts turn not to rage over the deaths of his friends or over his own possible death, or over the lack of social justice in South Texas. Instead:

> For me, there was the thought of home and friends, and,
> Strangely enough,
> > Of an Easter picnic near the river
> Where I met a girl named Nellie
> Now long dead and, I thought,
> Quite forgotten.
> > (*KLS,* p. 39)

The solution to the confusion of serving one's own oppressor is evidently not the assimilation to another world, but rather the determination to return to the contradictory, but familiar, one.

It is in the crucible of death which were the Korean battlefields that Rafa Buenrostro at mid-century, like Gregorio Cortez "with his pistol in his hand" in the early part of the twentieth century, resolves to take on the duty to live justly in Texas. Gregorio Cortez identifies himself in opposition to the Anglos who victimize him and his family. Rafa and others like him renew their solidarity by serving first as voluntary agents of American military power. The index of their song's ideology is thus not to be found first in its apparently innocent story, but in its ideological commitment to collective solidarity. No less surely than in *El Corrido de Gregorio Cortez*, the underlying symbolic impulse of *Korean Love Songs* turns out to be the resolution to reawaken in the midst of a privatizing and alienating dominant culture, even while half a world away, a continuing sense of the drive toward commmunity and collectivity which has been the historical heritage of the border communities of South Texas. Like their *corrido* folk art base, Rolando Hinojosa's "songs" thus align themselves with the most ideologically vital art forms of Mexican American culture. The songs serve to highlight and hold off the dissolving and fragmenting effects of contemporary American life while attempting to represent the conditions necessary for the retention of organic community life. It is a task which continues in symbolic form in his other exemplary works.

[1]Américo Paredes, "*With His Pistol in His Hand*": *A Border Ballad and its Hero* (Austin: University of Texas Press, 1958), p. 149. Hereafter cited by the author's name and by page number in parentheses in the body of the text.

[2]Rolando Hinojosa, *Korean Love Songs: From Klail City Death Trip* (Berkeley: Editorial Justa, 1978). All quotations are from this edition of the work and will be identified by the abbreviation *KLS* and page number in parentheses.

[3]Fredric Jameson, "Reification and Utopia in Mass Culture," *Social Text* 1 (1979): 130-148. Hereafter cited in the text by the author's name and by page number in parentheses.

[4]M. M. Bakhtin, *The Dialogic Imagination: Four Essays*, ed. Michael Holquist, trans. by Caryl Emerson and Michael Holquist (Austin: University of Texas Press, 1981), p. 209.

[5]Ramón Saldívar, "The Form of Texas Mexican Fiction," in *The Texas Literary Tradition: Fiction, Folklore, History*, eds. Don Graham, James W. Lee, and William T. Pilkington (Austin and The Texas State Historical Association, 1983), pp. 139-144.

[6]Of the several places where this issue is developed, the early formulation of the concept of the "division of labor" in Marx and Engels's *The German Ideology* (1845-46) is one of the most succinct. See *The German Ideology*, Part I in *The Marx-Engels Reader*, Second Edition, ed. by Robert C. Tucker (New York: W. W. Norton, 1978), p. 150. See also Herbert Marcuse's general introductory essay, "The Foundation of Historical Materialism" (1932), in *From Luther to Popper*, trans. Joris de Bres (London: *NLB*, Verso Editions, 1972;1983), pp. 1-48.

[7]Rolando Hinojosa, *Generaciones y semblanzas* (Berkeley: Justa Publications, 1977); published originally as *Klail City y sus alrededores* (La Habana: Casa de las Américas, 1976). Hereafter cited in the text by the abbreviation *GS*.

Margarita Cota-Cárdenas
Arizona State University

Mi querido Rafa and Irony: A Structural Study

Mi querido Rafa looms as Rolando Hinojosa's most realized achievement in the continuing, frequently critical and by turns delightful *opus magnus* created by the Chicano author.[1] In March, 1982, this novel was awarded the Southwest Conference on Latin American Studies (SCOLAS) prize for Best Writing in Humanities, 1981. Structured in the epistolar mode, it is the fifth work in a series subtitled *Klail City Death Trip* series. The reader's relationship to the text is essentially ironic, inasmuch as the reader is unaware of all the information possessed by the various characters. This knowledge/lack of knowledge relationship can vary so that the reader can shift from a "distant" to a "close" relationship with the narrator.[2] The reader's willingness to participate in the perceptibly programmed quest for knowledge about this fictional space — Klail City, Belken County, Texas — will largely determine the reader's ultimate enjoyment of the work.

Mi querido Rafa also serves as an excellent example of social commentary that does not have to alienate the reader to make a point. It is Hinojosa's controlled humor, through the use of multiple narrators, that is the key to this achievement.

Hinojosa expands and develops certain narrators and their narrative cycles introduced in his earlier "novellas". Such is the case in *Rafa,* where the narrative space is again the fictional Belken County, Texas, and the focus is again on the Buenrostro family and their Malacara cousins. But it is not only the *relato* (*what* is narrated) that will affirm for the reader the high regard for Hinojosa's work; it is also the *discurso (how* the narrator narrates, or in this case, speaks).[3] Enter then, the various narrative voices or ironic personae of the *Klail City Death Trip* series, of which the most notable are Rafa Buenrostro, Jehú Malacara, and P. Galindo.

The following could be said to be the character-Narrator P. Galindo's game plan: "Jehú Malacara has left Belken County under highly ambiguous circumstances, and you and I, dear reader, are to dig about and see what we can come up with. Perhaps it will even be close to the truth."

Mi querido Rafa is a *relato enmarcado,* a work that is contained within a framing level of narration.[4] In this instance, P. Galindo is the ironic fictitious narrator of the prologue at the beginning of Part I, "Malilla platicada" ("Gossip" or "Scuttlebutt") as well as of the epilogue following Part II, "Sondas y ciertos hallazgos de P. Galindo" ("Probes and Certain Discoveries by P. Galindo").

P. Galindo serves as a "dramatized narrator", that is to say, he is a character-narrator, but has few "vital", active characteristics as a person.[5] The reader's perception of this narrator must come forth through intellectual means, i.e., the narrator's discourse. Also, there are few references as to this narrator's physical person, although we do learn in Part II, "P. Galindo: *El Esc.*", that P. Galindo is unmarried, is 52 years of age, and has lived most of those years in Belken County.

P. Galindo constantly refers to himself as *el escritor* ("el esc.") and thus disavows any interference with the narratives that follow. His feigned detachment, of course, contributes to the ironic reading since what is said is juxtaposed against how it is said. In the prologue, for instance, the reader learns that Galindo has terminal skin cancer, was himself in the hospital with Rafa Buenrostro and that this is how Galindo obtained Jehú's letters to his cousin Rafa. The letters (Part I) and the account of Galindo's reportage (Part II) shall be his last contribution in the ongoing chronicle of Belken County. What Galindo says is that time and his own passing are of peripheral concern, and that what is important is what he is about to relate about Rafa and Jehú. The reader, however, savors the ironic, subtly revealing yet detached economy — that is, *el discurso*:

> Time, since we're talking about it, like anything —
> like all things, finishes; it disintegrates; it slithers away;
> it doesn't let anything get past it and more than marching

on, it packs up and runs. Somtimes, time stays there quietly and if one doesn't bother it nor pays attention to it,
time for its own part, will disappear. That, the piece
about not paying attention to it and about finishing and
disapppearing, is just like time.

Like I said. The *esc.*, then, has little time left (trans.,
p. 8)[6]

There is a restrained humor in the fictitious narrator's observations. Galindo, thus, appears to have this in common with
Jehú Malacara who is the narrator in Part I; Galindo, as I've
said, is the narrator/interviewer of Part II.

Part I, as Galindo shows the reader in the prologue, is constituted by the letters written by Jehú, a young Chicano working as
loan officer in the Bank in Klail City. The letters are adddressed
to Jehú's cousin, Rafa Buenrostro, a Korean War veteran who is
convalescing at the William Barrett, Texas, V.A. Hospital, some
miles away.

What the twenty-two letters in Part I relate, in essence, is
Jehú's gradual though inevitable involvement in Belken County
politics; this the reader perceives as Jehú's disillusionment
which leads to his ultimate alienation and his abrupt departure
from Klail. Jehú's letters — Galindo's protest to the contrary —
appear to filter through the same *perspectiva vital* as the basic
narrator's:[7]

> Ira Escobar was ready to pee his pants, he wanted so
> bad to blab it to somebody; that Noddy and some very
> important people, Jehú', had talked seriously with him,
> and etc., etc. In short, that the whole pack wanted Ira to
> try out for, or to run, as we say, for the post of commis-
> sioner of Precinct No. 4. You read it right, that's what he
> said. (trans., p. 9)

Jehú half-heartedly involves himself in the politicizing
through Noddy Perkins' machinations (vis á vis "the Ranch"),

although he does not support Escobar's candidacy privately. And then, suddenly Jehú falls in disfavor with Perkins, disappears, and becomes the subject of local gossip. The last letters to Rafa reflect Jehú's alienation, but the reader does not learn the possible reasons for Jehú's departure until Part II.

In the interviews/*sondeos* by Galindo, it is again not what is said but how it is said that matters. Each interview complements the knowledge acquired in the previous ones, but the most notable *sondeos* are those with Sammie Jo Perkins, Becky Escobar, Viola Barragán, Esther Lucille Bewley and Don Javier Leguizamón. The "truth" in Belken County lies amorphous in the interrelationship between *relato*/discurso — in brief, through what the reader must reconstruct.

The aforementioned characters are all interviewed in the book. The information given by Tapia, Jovita de Anda and others may be perceived as relatively minor in comparison to that obtained in the interviews with Viola Barragán, Becky Escobar, Sammie Jo Perkins, Esther Lucille Bewley, and Don Javier Leguizamón. It is from these that Galindo and the reader learns the following.

Viola Barragán:

Galindo interviews Barragán twice. She sides with Jehú and has, in fact, frequently encouraged Jehú to come work for her. Also, she has been privy to some information that Jehú had not told Rafa in the letters, principally about Jehú's relationship with Sammie Jo Perkins (pp. 64-65).

Barragán intimates that Noddy Perkins has told her of Jehú's conquest of Becky Escobar. She then wonders if this is the real reason for Jehu's departure from the Bank, or if it is Sammie Jo's sexual involvement with Jehú. The latter has apparently discovered the homosexual relationship between Sammie Jo's husband Sydney, and Hap Bayliss, one of Noddy Perkins' cronies and a deposed congressman.

In any case, Barragán expresses open admiration for Jehú, a contrast to the prevailing attitude among the town's Chicanos who openly criticize Jehú's departure from the Bank.

Esther Lucille Bewley:

Galindo describes her quite sympathetically despite his avowed objectivity; Bewley absolutely discredits the talk that Jehú is guilty of any sort of misconduct. She is certain people know the truth and where he has gone. Furthermore, Bewley has witnessed Jehú's encounter with Noddy Perkins, prior to Jehú's departure. He puts Noddy in the difficult position of having to retain Jehú because — according to Esther Lucille — Jehú has outwitted Perkins (pp. 105-106).

Without Bewley's introspection, we could not get this particular witness-account of the encounter at the Bank. Her frankness allows new information to filter to Galindo, and therefore to the reader.

Becky Escobar:

What is revealing about Becky's interview, is what she does *not* say to Galindo. She claims that she and Ira had an acquaintanceship with Jehú, but disclaims any knowledge of Jehú's personal affairs. In fact, the whole town appears to be gossiping that Jehú has indeed had "an affair" with Ira Escobar's wife. Since Jehú admits to Perkins what he has hinted at in his letters to Rafa about Becky Escobar, it is unlikely that Perkins did not know. Becky is cast in an ironic light, inasmuch as she pretends that her relationship with Jehú was highly impersonal while Galindo — and the reader — know this to be to the contrary. Becky does not know that Galindo knows.

Sammie Jo Perkins:

The reader, like the narrator P. Galindo, may well feel admiration for this character's directness. She shares this trait with Viola Barragán, and like Barragán, Sammie Jo bluntly denies the theory of any financial wrongdoing by Jehú. Sammie Jo, however, reveals that she may have been generous in her admiration of the Malacara-Buenrostro clan, when she hints to Galindo about her own relationship in the past with Rafa. The narrator Galindo chooses — typically — not to press this last piece of information further. However, while Galindo professes not to hasten to any conclusions as to Jehú's, Rafa's and Sammie Jo's "history", he does "protest too much."

> The reader can't help but notice that Jehú is neither a saint nor a devil. Now, that the truth should come out of Sammie Jo's mouth is the biggest of ironies. The *esc.* thinks that Sammie Jo knows that Rafa doesn't answer telephones like that, casually, because of Jehú. The *esc.* doesn't see any other connection. (trans., p. 76)

We might note that while some questions are answered, there are many inferences made which raise other questions. Exactly in the manner of "scuttlebutt or gossip," the following questions develop in Part II: Is it about Sammie Jo's promiscuity or is it because Jehú found her husband's locket, a gift from his male lover (the old *politico* Bayliss who was unseated by Roger Terry, as planned and executed by Noddy Perkins), that Jehú raises Perkins' ire?

Interestingly, Perkins says in his own interview (Chapter 32) that he knows that Jehú was not above seducing Becky Escobar, but that he considered that to be bank business, if it had happened, although he won't say that he knows the seduction to be a fact. In fact, Perkins does know (see Part I, Chapter 19).[8] Perkins does not admit nor refer to Jehú's seeing Sammie Jo at Perkins' ranch, where the episode with Sydney's locket is supposed to have occurred. Perkins does reveal one item of information available to Galindo, and that is about Viola Barragán and Gela Maldonado, Leguizamón's girlfriend. Acording to Perkins, they were old flames from Perkins' youth and Perkins can relate to Jehú's possible amours. In any case, Galindo's reaction to this last information is tempered yet humorous:

Confession: The *esc.* smoked one of the cigars Perkins offered him and paid for it with two days in bed, he was so sick from it.

The *esc.* advises the reader that he didn't know nor had any inkling of the old Perkins-Barragán and Perkins-Maldonado connections. The *esc.* will only permit himself to say that anything's possible . . . (trans., p. 78).

Don Javier Leguizamón:

This character is a distant relative by marriage of Ira Escobar. He helped Ira obtain his position at the Bank, and he claims some influence in having helped Jehú likewise.

Don Javier is highly disliked by most of "la raza", but he remains a powerful figure with influence at "the Ranch".[9] It appears that Jehú might have crossed Leguizamón and Perkins in a land deal, "beat them to the gun" by going to "la raza" and telling them what these two old cronies were up to.

Although Galindo does not make his usual commentaries as to content of the interview, he does allow the reader to perceive his true opinion of this pompous character: "*El esc.* prefers that what was said by J. L. remain his personal, inviolable, untouchable monument" (trans., p. 108).

The Epilogue:

In the pithy epilogue, it is also what is referred to yet left unsaid that "fills in the spaces". The "*malilla platicada*" is exactly what goes on in the streets. "*Por esas cosas que pasan*" translates: "because of the way things happen" and means that we are getting a subjective view of what has happened in spite of the filtering through a supposedly objective perspective by Galindo.

Galindo says in this last section, that if Jehú were to return to Klail, "even the dogs would line up to pee on him" (p. 112). In other words, Jehú is in general disfavor, with few exceptions, and only among the "real raza" is he still held in good opinion.[10]

Although many profess to having "information" that is reliable, most either ignore the truth or choose to deny it. Of the interviews, thirteen are favorably inclined to Jehú's character, and ten are negative.[11]

The mosaic technique calls for "filling in the spaces". The episodes in Part I must be related by the reader to any new information gathered in Part II. The expansion of a particular character is made possible in Part II through the interviews. In this manner, then, contrasts and similarities are established.[12]

This technique requires that the reader's role be an active one in the ironic reconstructions. Clearly, the reader must reconstruct what has happened to tie the loose narrative threads. The narrator Galindo gives sufficient hints as to his own inclination in accepting or ignoring or rejecting pieces of information.

For example, the episode between Jehú and Sammie Jo at Perkins's Ranch is first related by Jehú in his letter (Chapter 7) to Rafa. It is, however, only summarily mentioned (p. 22), and the reader is given more information in subsequent chapters/interviews by Barragán and Sammie Jo. But this episode is later hilariously "filled-in" in "Eugenio & Isidro Peralta, Cuates", (Chapter 38 pp. 92-94). The twin brothers interviewed here reveal that indeed, Jehú has seduced Sammie Jo, and indeed, Sammie Jo has previously been involved with Rafa Buenrostro. The twins' double-talk astounds the narrator Galindo, and the entire interview would indeed be hilarious if the narrator's restraint would allow it.

One should also consider two other relationships: the reader to Jehú, Part I, and the reader to Galindo, Part II. Also, the perspective of diegetic, metadiegetic discourse might be considered in a more in-depth study of *Rafa*.[13] In any case, Jehú's discourse bears strong resemblance to that of Galindo, as has been previously indicated. Galindo's commentary is sparse in comparison to Jehú's succinct letters, but as we have said in the beginning of this study, they appear to share the same "*perspectiva vital*".

Overall, the reader develops his/her perception of the narrator Galindo as an ironic one. We could consider if the relationship of the narrator to his/her subject is superior, inferior or on an equal plane. The narrator Galindo does not idealize nor does he moralize; although he appears not to interfere, there clearly is an ironic effect. The "ironic reconstruction" as illustrated by Wayne Booth, implies that what is said and what is understood may not be, upon further (and ironic) reconstruction by the listener/reader, what is really meant.[14] Therefore, we might consider what kind of reader is actually required in the reading of *Rafa*. What are his/her beliefs? What about the "ideal reader's" cultural/political make-up?[15] Are there limitations or possibilities in the projection of such a reader, for the "ideal reading" of *Mi querido Rafa*? Without attempting to address specifically these questions here, we might still offer the following conclusions.

Belken County — with all its political intrigue, racism, and hypocrisy — can still overpower and even alienate the Hinojosa Chicano-Antihero-Everyman, but the deadpan humor serves Hinojosa's narrator to endure an often intolerable Chicano reality.

The reader is left to consider if Jehú "did right" by leaving Klail. How can this character sustain his integrity in such an environment? Ira Escobar does not, nor does Leguizamón. We are to believe that, in part, these other characters do not have the same values/ethics as Jehú. Still, they are not the only ones in Klail to appear to "give over" some portion of their personal beliefs or in fact to "sell out."

The interesting and important aspect of the narrator's restraint is that he is, in fact, to a great degree non-judgmental. The humor inherent in his world-view indeed appears to make bearable some very serious defects in the smug status quo of Belken County. We are given all the options available, even those carried to simplistic solutions. Given such a frustrating, overpowering and corrupt environment and the overwhelmingly racist, fickle or uninformed general population, one can survive by 1) co-opting, as does Ira Escobar; 2) selling out, like Roger Terry; 3) maintaining the status quo, like Javier Leguizamón and Noddy Perkins; or 4) refusing to participate, or perhaps even leaving Belken, like Olivia San Esteban, Jehú's girlfriend, and like Jehú. In Jehú's case, he chooses apparently — this is not entirely clear, as we have previously indicated — to leave Klail City rather than to continue to compromise his ethics.

We must consider Jehú representative of a Chicano Everyman, because he is not idealized nor is he of "heroic" dimensions. He is sexually imprudent, although we hasten to add that he fully chooses to be so and therefore we must not mistake this as some "tragic defect" leading to his downfall. Klail City is not, according to Galindo, neither more hypocritical nor less intriguing than all of Belken County, or Texas.

The ironic condition of the Chicano antihero in *Mi querido Rafa* is one which is indeed deadly, intolerable, and yet which is somehow lived.[16] If there exists a generic Noddy Perkins ("The Ranch") with all his historically entrenched machinations, then, so are there also a Viola Barragán, an Olivia San Esteban, a Jehú Malacara — and a P. Galindo.

Finally, if the reader is familiar with Hinojosa's insights in his previous multiple perspectives on this fictional clan, then he/she will delight in the reading of *Rafa*. The painful Chicano "space" reconstructed therein will negatively effect some readers. Nonetheless, Hinojosa's narrators' use of humor is, to this reader, mostly hopeful rather than cynical. *Como lees.*[17]

[1]Rolando Hinojosa, *Mi querido Rafa* (Houston: Arte Público Press, 1981); hereafter referred to as *Rafa*.

[2]Wayne Booth says, "In any reading experience there is an implied dialogue among author, narrator, the other characters, and the reader. Each of the four can range, in relation to each of the others, from identification to complete opposition, on any axis of value, moral, intellectual, aesthetic, and even physical." *Rhetoric of Fiction* (Chicago: University of Chicago Press, 1961), p. 155.

[3]I am relying on Tzvetan Todorov's discussion of "story and discourse" (*relato* and *discurso*) in "Las categorías del relato literario," *Comunica-*

ciones 8: análisis estructural del relato (Buenos Aires: Tiempo Contempor neo, 1972), pp. 155-192.

[4]"A story within a frame," the *relato enmarcado* has such distinguished antecedents as Cervantes' *Don Quijote* and José Eustasio Rivera's *La vorágine* (1924). This second novel is also a scathing indictment of the exploitation and annihilation of man in the Colombian rubber industry. The main characters are literally vanquished by their "space", the Colombian jungle.

[5]Wayne Booth says that "In a sense even the most reticent narrator has been dramatized as soon as he refers to himself as 'I' . . .", *op.cit.*, p. 152. P. Galindo is not as fully dramatized as, say, Jehú in Part I. We might even say that compared to Jehú, P. Galindo is "non-dramatized". See Booth's discussion of "non-dramatized" and "dramatized" narrators, *op.cit.*, pp. 151-153.

[6]All the translations from *Rafa* are mine.

[7]This is the "vital perspective" of the basic narrator, i.e. his "world's view" or *weltanschauung*.

[8]In Chapter 19, Jehú confronts Noddy Perkins and asks: "Does my firing have to do with sex, Noddy?" He then admits to an affair with Becky Escobar but denies a relationship with Sammie Jo, pp. 46-47.

[9]In Chapter 34, Rufino Fischer Gutiérrez says of Ira Escobar's candidacy for Commissioner: "When we found out here that a Leguizamón (Escobar) was going to run for commissioner over there, the *Mexicanos* from this county saw this as a move to grab more land. We weren't far from the truth.", (trans., p. 82).

[10]These would be those that have not "co-opted", given over or embraced the *modus operandi* of Leguizamón and Perkins. This delineation of a particular social class and the concomitant world's view might be fruitfully studied from a "genetic structuralist" perspective such as Lucien Goldmann's; according to Terry Eagleton, "Goldmann is concerned to examine the structure of a literary text for the degree to which it embodies the structure of thought (or 'world vision') of the social class or group to which the writer belongs. The more closely the text approximates to a complete, coherent articulation of the social class's 'world vision', the greater is its validity as a work of art.", *Marxism and Literary Criticism* (Berkeley and Los Angeles: University of California Press, 1976), p. 32.

[11]One interview is Galindo's (Chapter 37) own, and although he continues to avow objectivity, he is disposed in favor of Jehú: "For now we can say that he left the post of his own will no matter what is said among *la raza* up to now . . .", (trans. p. 90). Two of the "positive" interviews are Viola Barragán's.

[12]*Mise en abyme* is an extreme example of the thematic function of a metadiegetic narrative, whereby analogy verges on identity; the metadiegetic narrative can also have an explicative function so that the inner narrative becomes an explanation of the outer. *Mise en abyme* establishes relations of

contrast and similarity between diegesis and metadiegesis. See Shlomith Rimmon, "A Comprehensive Theory of Narrative: Genette's *Figures III* and the Structuralist Study of Fiction," *PTL* 1:1 (1976), p. 53.

[13]These terms are from Gerard Genette, *Figures III* (Paris: Seuil, 1972). The diegetic level of narration is the level of the primary narrative or the primary fictional events; the metadiegetic are narrative levels contained within other narrative levels. The extradiegetic level would be the framing level of narration (P. Galindo's prologue and epilogue) and external to the primary fictional events. P. Galindo's Interviews, Part II, would be the diegetic level; and Jehu's letters to Rafa would be the metadiegetic level which explains, elaborates, or is contrasted with the diegetic level.

[14]Booth speaks of the deconstructive and reconstructive nature of irony and describes two main categories of irony. Stable irony generally requires one or two reconstructions, but unstable irony requires many reconstructions. See Booth's *Rhetoric of Irony* (Chicago: University of Chicago Press, 1974), pp. 257-269.

[15]This "Ideal Reader" is to some critics a projection of the implied author or basic narrator, an implied version of "himself", and in writing a particular kind of book, a special kind of reader is created: "To write one kind of book is always to some extent a repudiation of other kinds. And regardless of an author's professed indifference to the reader, every book carves out from mankind those readers for which its peculiar effects were designed.", Booth, *Rhetoric of Fiction*, p. 136.

[16]Charles Glicksberg says, "The heart of irony is to be found in a contradiction which cannot be resolved and which cannot be endured and yet which is somehow lived," *The Ironic Vision in Modern Literature* (The Hague: Martinus Nijhoff, 1969), p. 258.

[17]"You read it right, that's what I said." I am repeating a laconic expression of Jehú's from Chapter 1, Part 1 (p. 9), as a manner of emphasizing the particular tone taken by Hinojosa's narrators in *Rafa*.

Lauro Flores
University of Washington

Narrative Strategies in Rolando Hinojosa's *Rites and Witnesses*

I have proposed elsewhere that Rolando Hinojosa-Smith's overall narrative project departs from a fundamental premise: the tension and dynamics that exist between the unfolding of individual (personal) and collective (group) history.[1]

Viewing these opposite elements not as mutually antagonistic contradictions but, more precisely, as two interacting poles of a single whole, the author consciously or unconsciously assumes this conflict from the outset and skillfully shapes it into his fiction. Yet, as I have suggested before, what seems to prevail or to be more important in his works in the final analysis is the collectivity, not the individual.

At least two essential aspects of Hinojosa's narrative derive from the above postulate: 1) the absence of a well-defined protagonist ("hero"), and 2) the *collage* format on which all of his works published to date are structurally arranged.

While these and some of the other traits discussed later on in this essay became evident immediately after the publication of his first two books, *Estampas del valle y otras obras* (1973), and *Klail City y sus alrededores/Generaciones y semblanzas* (1976-77), it was necessary to wait for Hinojosa's subsequent works not only to accurately verify the theorem proposed at the beginning of these notes, but also to be able to fully visualize the evolution of the problem and the narrative strategies that the author had to adopt in order to better contend with it in his fiction.[2] In this sense, *Rites and Witnesses* appears to be a concentrated sample in which we find well condensed Hinojosa's style, technical abilities and thematic preoccupations.[3] Its analysis, therefore, should contribute to the elucidation of immediate meaning of this novel and also should enhance the understanding of the writer's general endeavor.

Since the publication of *Estampas* and *Generaciones,* Hinojosa's writing activity has evolved into a continuous project now known as the *Klail City Death Trip series.* The other works making up the series are: *Korean Love Songs* (1978), the poetic installment of the sequence; *Claros varones de Belken,* a novel due to appear shortly; and *Mi querido Rafa* (1981), an epistolary novel that, chronologically at least, constitutes the immediate antecedent to *Rites and Witnesses.*[4]

Hinojosa's fictional universe revolves around Klail City, a mythical town in the Río Grande Valley of Texas, and includes various other places of imaginary Belken and Dellis counties (Flora, Bascom, Edgerton, Relámpago, Jonesville-on-the-River, etc). This microcosm, besides its unquestionable aesthetic qualities, constitutes a veritable chronicle of the social, political, economic, and linguistic realities that have operated for many generations in the Anglo/Chicano world of the Rio Grande Valley.

Within this context, *Rites and Witnesses* emerges not only as a commendable work of fiction but perhaps as Hinojosa's most enjoyable book so far. Thematically and stylistically, it continues to build the mosaic initiated by the author in *Estampas.* This dimension of continuity is reinforced, as we will see, by the numerous characters appearing in the novel, many of whom we have already met or glimpsed at in previous works.

It must be admitted, then, that to fully comprehend the underlying meaning of *Rites and Witnesses,* this book has to be viewed in its proper context — i.e., as a piece of the larger puzzle to which it rightfully belongs. This does not mean, however, that the novel lacks autonomy. Neither does it mean that the uninformed reader should be incapable of understanding the immediate plot, the internal dynamics of the story, or of enjoying the clear and precise style, the irony and the humor which by now are widely recognized as the fundamental trademark of Hinojosa's prose.

A further word of caution is needed here as many readers will undoubtedly tend to confuse continuity with repetition. In proposing that Hinojosa's narrative gravitates around a central and constant premise, in saying that his characters, style, and technical resources remain consistent throughout the six titles presently making up his series, I do not mean to imply that his prose is redundant or that it lacks diversity or imagination. On the contrary, Hinojosa's writing resembles the task of a cubist painter who studies his subject matter from a variety of angles and whose works' complexity can only be understood upon a simultaneous reading of the work in its entirety. As such, Hinojosa's artistic undertaking obviously represents an ambitious attempt to exhaustively explore the multiple facets of a rich, complex, and problematic reality and to render as faithfully as possible a portrait of it to the reader. His fiction, then, is not a mechanical repetition of motifs or narrative resources but an ingenious development of a coherent literary project.

Hinojosa's writing must be understood, therefore, as a chronicle-like endeavor in which the author attempts to grasp the intricacies of his society in an "objective" fashion. In doing so, for example, he makes a deliberate effort to avoid idealizing the characters he creates. Instead, he aims at presenting them as people really are, with all their virtues and faults.[5]

Aside from developing a plot and a network of characters congruent with such a premise, the writer's immediate task has been to identify and adopt the narrative devices that would allow him to incorporate into his fiction the dynamics of that reality, as he understands them, and also to nurture it with a strong dose of realism.

The central question, however, still remains. How does the author view reality, how does he convey it to the reader, and which are those narrative strategies that he has utilized in order to create a fictional world that corresponds to his particular vision of the world?

Following up on my initial statements, I will propose here that, whereas the previously mentioned tension between the individual and the collective does constitute indeed the main motor behind Hinojosa's fiction, this tension is incorporated by the author into his works not as a truly dynamic motion but rather as a static relationship between two opposing forces that coexist and finally neutralize each other. Aesthetically, this process results in a well-balanced combination of narrative elements and techniques, as I expect to demonstrate here. The key concept to understanding Hinojosa's seemingly dismembered and, at times, contradictory universe is equilibrium.

In *Rites and Witnesses,* as it occurs in other novels by the author, this equilibrium is transferred into other aspects of the book (plot, characters, structure) and thus ceases to be a tacit thematic assumption in order to become a dominant and graphically explicit element of the narration.

Consistent with the dualistic approach and the maintenance of equilibrium, for example, the plot of *Rites and Witnesses* is made up of two parallel and alternating actions, each unfolding in a different spatial and temporal frame. The immediate events take place in Klail City in the course of a few months of the year 1959, and basically depict the lifestyle and the secret and open manipulations of the local banking and ranching barons, whose aims are to increase the economic and political control they have been amassing in the Valley for generations — generally at the expense of the Chicanos (through the violation of original land grants, for example), but also with the cooperation and complicity of some of them (Viola Barragán, Polín Tapia, and Javier Leguizamón among others), as we soon find out.

Similarly, it should be noted that this first set of actions also unfolds on two separate substages: the Bank and the Klail-Blanchard-Cooke Ranch (the KBC), both natural domains of these powerful families. The central figure in these occurrences, nonetheless, is Jehú Malacara, a Chicano who despite his employment in the Bank refuses to participate in the political game of the ruling group. Throughout this section of the novel, Hinojosa does not waste any opportunity to outline in a subtle and sarcastic tone the vices and decadence of this social elite: Blanche Cooke's alcoholism; Sammie Jo Perkins' nymphomania; Sidney Boynton's homosexual relationship with Hap Bayliss, his godfather and a U.S. Representative; and Sanford Blanchard's ("El Borrachín") sexual exploitation of Mexican and Central American maids such as Nicéfora Cruz.

173

The second line of events unfolds in Korea nine years earlier and seemingly occupies a full year — from late 1950 through September of 1951. The main actor here is Rafa Buenrostro, a cousin of Jehú Malacara. Rafa is wounded in action twice and ultimately becomes another of the nearly forgotten war heroes. The last page of the novel, quite significantly, is supposed to be a facsimile of the Army report containing the official version of the second incident in which Rafa is injured and several of his comrades are killed.

The duality embodied in the last names of these two characters ("Goodface" — "Badface," literally translated) is painfully obvious.[6] In addition, both Rafa Buenrostro and Jehú Malacara, as we know, have been evolving as "protagonists" in Hinojosa's project since the initial works of the series. The first half of *Mi querido Rafa*, for example, is organized around a succession of letters written by Jehú to Rafa when the first one is working at the bank (presumably the immediate present of *Rites and Witnesses*) and the latter is in the William Barrett Veterans' Administration Hospital, still suffering from his old war wounds. In essence, then, more than an "antecedent," which in a strict publication order it really is, *Mi querido Rafa* turns out to be the document in which we find the key to the outcome of the political conflicts and intrigues we encounter in *Rites and Witnesses*.

Also conforming with the equilibrium game conducted by the author, the formal and technical aspects of this novel continue to reflect Hinojosa's narrative skill and aesthetic preoccupations. The book is structurally divided into thirty-five small "chapters" (each is one to five pages in length) and distributed between two almost symmetrical parts. The first half, appropriately subtitled "The Rites," encompasses chapters one through sixteen (pp. 7-64), while the second half, "The Witnesses," carries us through the last nineteen chapters (pp. 65-112).

Clearly, the "rites" are the actions performed by the individuals who comprise the different human groups populating Hinojosa's world, the Mexicans in the Valley and the rank and file soldiers in Korea. Due to their simple character, these deeds often remain unnoticed and seem to matter only to those individuals directly involved in them. However, and this seems to be the novelist's main point of contention, the ordinary or heroic nature of the incidents is subject to interpretation. In Hinojosa we find distilled a number of unsung, stoic heroes whose actions are part of a collective history and, insofar as this is true, mold such history in the long run. Placed in this context, the second of the three epigraphs utilized by Hinojosa at the beginning of his books becomes fully relevant:

> His means of death, his obscure burial
> No trophy, sword, nor hatchment o'er his bones,
> No noble rite nor formal ostentation.

The "witnesses," on the other hand, are the people themselves whose accounts the writer pretends to merely collect, record, and save for posterity. Given this posture, one could safely assume that the omniscient narrator, if not the author himself, also becomes part of the witnesses. Thus, the separation between these two groups (rites and witnesses) seems almost artificial as they are one and the same.

In the Korean setting, the witnesses, quite literally, are those men whose accounts force Captain Bracken, the biased Army officer, to confer Rafa with a bronze medal instead of court-martialing him as was his original intention: "He (Sgt. Hatalsky), ah, says, that, you, ah, y-you did a fine thing; you've got five witnesses . . . that's probably three more than you need . . ." (p. 79).[8]

The Chicanos' "heroic" role in the configuration of the history of Belken County, on the other hand, is conveyed by word of mouth by those ten witnesses (nine Angloamericans and one Chicano), who take turns presenting their visions of the Valley Mexicans. Excluding Abel Manzano's rendering, such views range from a sympathetic, almost paternalistic outlook which presents Mexicans as "really grateful," "apppreciative," "hard working, long suffering and loyal as anything," i.e., as servile individuals (p.90), to a chauvinistic position which depicts them as a "bunch-a goddam-ingrates" (p. 76) who are "worse than niggers" (p. 97). Manzano's account, very significantly, is the last one in the book. This is meaningful because he has the last word and also because he, a Valley Mexican, voices his opinion and makes an attempt at interpreting his people's reality. It is interesting to note that while most of his comments are made from a first person singular point of view, in the closing part of his remarks he adopts a plural point of view: "He (Choche Markham) knows the way we feel; the way we act." (p. 111).

In this novel, as in Hinojosa's previous works, the main structural device is a multiperspective presentation of the material. Thus, the *collage* character of his narrative is preserved. It seems almost unnecessary to point out that the author's pretended role as a gatherer of accounts is a deliberate attempt on his part to surround the story with a halo of verisimilitude. Using techniques very much like those utilized by writers throughout history (Cervantes, Borges, etc.), Hinojosa successfully commands the attention of the reader and makes an effort to obliterate the distance between fiction and reality, thereby enhancing the documentary character of his works. Among the most commmonly used of the techniques that Hinojosa has been exploiting since his early writings, we find editors' and translators' footnotes, newspaper excerpts, transcriptions of recorded conversations, and official documents such as legal depositions or the one-page Army report which closes *Rites and Witnesses.*[7]

The near absence of descriptive narration, of direct narration in general, and the heavy reliance on monologue and dialogue endow the novel with an extreme agility and a theatrical quality which make the action flow quite easily and turn the reading into a very enjoyable exercise. This theatrical technique is exemplified by the laconic interventions of the third person omniscient narrator in the opening lines of chapters nine and fourteen: "At the KBC. Poolside." (p. 39) "Jehú's office. On top of the desk: a number of previously approved loan applications awaiting a signature." (p. 54). Needless to say, the monologues also facilitate the development of the psychology and motivations of the characters. Outstanding in this respect are the interior monologues held by Polín Tapia, the opportunist Chicano newsmonger (p. 22) and Sammie Jo Perkins, the spoiled and frustrated daughter of Noddy Perkins, the bank president (p. 47).

Contrary to most of Hinojosa's works, *Rites and Witnesses* is written in English. This is necessary because the actions take place in environments where the Angloamerican presence is dominant: the Army and the bank. But, in addition, this is also characteristic of the author's continuous and meticulous efforts to give his narrative a realistic tone.

The linguistic sphere has consistently been an arena where we find clearly expressed the tension and dynamics between the two main groups in Hinojosa's fiction, Anglos and Chicanos. Consequently, language is also used in *Rites and Witnesses* to illustrate the influence that Mexicans have had on the *bolillos* (Anglos). Most of them, even the very rich and powerful ones, speak Spanish ("Tex-Mex") to some degree. It is indeed Noddy Perkins' ability to speak Spanish and his willingness to interact with the Mexicans that have made possible his central role in the business of that elite he joined by marrying Blanche Cooke: "Neither Ibby (Cooke) nor Junior Klail would mix with the Mexicans. That much, anyway . . . Noddy would. For business reasons. But he would, and so, the KBC, unable to fail or to flounder, was steered, locally, by Noddy." (p. 35). Ironically, however, he has never achieved complete acceptance in the midst of this circle: "Noddy is not family; he's necessary; he's a hard worker; he sees things through; etc. But it was that everlasting BUT HE'S NOT F." (p. 35).

I initiated this discussion by reasserting my proposition that the tension between the group and the individual constitutes the main basis for the development of Hinojosa's fiction. At first sight, one might be tempted to argue that this tension is ultimately reconciled through the writing activity of the author as the final outcome of his activity — the book itself — graphically "synthesizes" them together. A close look at the text, however, will show that the tension is statically captured in the writing, almost as a series of snapshots, that it remains there as such, and that it is left up to the reader to provide the final and perhaps subconscious solution to the dilemma.

Properly analyzed, then, this contradiction does not appear in Hinojosa's novels as a dialectical operation, as one might perceive it to be upon a quick reading. Insofar as no real synthesis or resolution of the conflict is provided at the conclusion of the narration, this vision, as objective and materialist as it is, resembles more a dualistic view of the world than a dialectical motion. Consequently, what we confront in Hinojosa's novels is a process in which two elements face each other and neutralize each other at the same time. The result is a carefully calculated equilibrium between the two.

With *Rites and Witnesses,* Hinojosa renders yet another facet of that microcosm he has been building bit by bit as a monumental project aimed at interpreting that reality of the Río Grande Valley he knows so well. This book meets quite well the literary goals he has set with his previous works and continues to credit him as the most prolific and perhaps most important contemporary Chicano writer.

[1]"The quotidian hero in the Chicano novel," a paper read at the MLA convention held in Los Angeles, California, December, 1982.

[2]This, Hinojosa's second book, was awarded the Casa de las Américas Prize for Best Spanish American Novel in 1976 and was originally published in Cuba with the first title. The following year, a bilingual version of the novel appeared in the United States under the new title of *Generaciones y semblanzas.*

[3](Houston: Arte Público Press, 1982). All references and page numbers in this essay correspond to this edition.

[4]Arte Público Press has recently announced *Partners in Crime,* a "tale of international intrigue and mystery," as the author's latest title. In addition, *The Valley* and *Dear Rafe,* Hinojosa's English recreations of his first and fifth novels are also available to the reader.

[5]I have elaborated further on this matter in my study cited in note 1 above. The author himself makes this point quite clearly in the first page of *Generaciones y semblanzas* (Berkeley: Justa Publications, 1977).

[6]This and other points regarding the role of these characters are also included in my previous paper.

[7]This type of narrative exercise is used exacerbatedly by Hinojosa in his short piece "Por esas cosas que pasan."

[8]The language used here is reminiscent of the third epigraph used by the author to open the novel: "In the mouth of two or three witnesses shall every word be established."

José David Saldívar
University of Houston

Our Southwest:
An Interview with Rolando Hinojosa

José Saldívar: Rolando, why don't we begin by talking about the evolution of your work? In your essay "A Voice of One's Own," you say that your first paid publication appeared in the Spring 1972 issue of *El Grito*. Can you tell us about the evolution of your project *Klail City Death Trip*, as you see it?

Rolando Hinojosa: The very first thing for which I got paid is "Por esas cosas que pasan." I wanted to write a bilingual piece. I was also very interested at the time — as I still am — in perspective, and I wanted a first-person perspective by Balde, and by the other characters as well. When I wrote that, I was much impressed by Tomás Rivera's . . . *y no se lo tragó la tierra*. I too had been trying to publish in Spanish in the United States for a long time, but I'd been unable to do so. I just couldn't find a place for it. I hadn't come up with the idea of a *Klail City Death Trip* as yet when I wrote that piece. But, I had so much material to write, that I knew it was going to be a matter of sitting down and doing it. But the impetus for my project comes from "Por esas cosas que pasan." Once it is published, I said, I'll write another piece: "Una vida de Rafa Buenrostro." Tomás Rivera read it first, by the way. I then wrote "Vidas y milagros" and "Estampas." Then, I collected all four pieces and sent them off to Quinto Sol Publications, for I now had the formation of a book. I was awarded the Premio Quinto Sol immediately after Rudy Anaya had won his for *Bless me, Ultima*. During the publication of *Estampas del valle y otras obras* (the title chosen by Octavio Romano and Herminio Ríos) I was already writing *Klail City y sus alrededores*. It wasn't called that then, you understand. This second book had a strange genesis.

I first wrote "Notas de Klail City y sus Alrededores, II" and I attached it to another brief piece "Brechas Viejas y Nuevas." The third piece was called "Generaciones y semblanzas." So, I was going to call the book: *Notas, Generaciones y Brechas*, using those three terms. I submitted the manuscript to Casa de las Américas because I had received notice of their contest. I knew the history of the Cuban publishing house, of course; and I also knew of the outstanding record of the people they had published. But I had no idea I could enter. So I wrote them a tentative letter — mail takes forty-five days, or it did in those days, between us and Cuba. I wrote them explaining my status as a Chicano, an American Citizen of Mexican descent. I also informed them that I was sending them the manuscript by separate mail. Let me explain what I did: I didn't send the manuscript directly to Cuba because I knew it would take forever to get there. Instead, I sent the manuscript to their maildrop in Switzerland — it got there in less than a week. I was living in Kingsville, Texas, at the time of the writing. Well, lo and behold, in 1976, February, I received a letter announcing the prize and I also received a telegram on the same date. Strange, isn't it?

After the completion of the novel, I had hit a six or seven-month fallow field. I was reading, though, and I'd gone from Chairman to Dean, and that took time away as well. I was Dean when the prize came through; about a year or so later, I was Vice President for Academic Affairs and then, for personal reasons (the personal reason being that my wife wanted to go to graduate school; subsequently, she became an attorney), I moved up to the University of Minnesota. And, it was there that I wrote and Justa Publications published *Korean Love Songs*. By now, the idea of a *Klail City Death Trip* was absolutely fixed. With the publication of *Korean Love Songs,* the project title *Klail City Death Trip* first appears in print. It went into two printings — which isn't bad for a book of poetry. This was written in English: the reason for that was I had originally tried to write about Korea in Spanish, but that experience wasn't lived in Spanish. Army life isn't conducted in Spanish, as you know. So, when I began writing *Korean Love Songs* in narrative prose and in English, it was easier. But it wasn't what I wanted, either. Eventually, after reading many of the British World War I poets, I got the idea that maybe I should use poetry to render something as brutal as war. That, then, is why I wrote *Korean Love Songs* in verse and in

English.

Then, *Claros varones de Belken* came around. I wanted to use the same format I had used for *Estampas* and for *Klail City* in the writing of *Claros varones*.

It was accepted for publication by Justa, but not published. The contracts were signed, but Justa Publications suffered some reversals . . . y allí se quedó. Nothing was done with it.

After that, I wrote the epistolary book *Mi querido Rafa.* Now, of course, I had placed both Jehú and Rafa in their thirties — post-Army, post-University days, and in the business world. It seemed to me very natural that if you were going to be working in business — which is the Anglo world *par excellance* — that the English language would now have to be invading the territory as far as usage was concerned. So, *Mi querido Rafa* is bilingual, and in the Jehú to Rafa letters, Jehú uses both languages, although English will predominate eventually. When I did the reportage part of the novel, which is the second part to *Mi querido Rafa,* I assigned English to some characters, Spanish to others, and a mixture of both to different generations.

And after that novel came *Rites and Witnesses* and the other material.

José Saldívar: Can you talk briefly about your new material?

Rolando Hinojosa: I've talked long and hard with some people, but primarily with Luis Leal, at different functions and conferences, about *Mi querido Rafa.* What I wanted to do, I told him, was to do what I'd been doing with *Estampas del valle*; as you know, I re-created — recast — *Estampas* and called it *The Valley.* It is a complete re-creation. In fact, some of the foci change as well. Don Luis told me that one could not translate the bilingual text, because all one could do was to translate from one language to another all over again. I disagreed gently, because I was interested in how the work would turn out. So, I have now re-created *Mi querido Rafa* the way I re-created *Estampas.* I submitted *Dear Rafe* to Nicolás Kanellos and Arte Público Press, and it was accepted. As to *Claros varones de Belken,* Gary Keller of Bilingual Press wanted it and had asked for it two or three years before. I finally relented and gave it to him. I understand that he has assigned a fine translator — Julia Cruz — for it.

After *Mi querido Rafa,* I had already talked to Nicolás Kanellos in Mexico City about some notes I was collecting. Rafa was now thirty-five, thirty-six or seven, . . . oh, incidentally, he had been widowed since he was eighteen or nineteen years old — something few readers know because *Claros varones* hasn't been published yet. But I knew what Rafa's life was like and I decided to make him an attorney.

As an undergraduate at the University of Texas at Austin, Rafa Buenrostro had been a Spanish major. Upon graduation, he had gone on to Law School at U.T. Austin. In *Mi querido Rafa,* if you will recall, Rafa was at the Veterans' Hospital in William Barrett, Texas. As I worked on *Dear Rafe* and thought about a new work, the one I mentioned to Nicolás, I asked myself: why did I put him in the V.A. Hospital in the first place? Maybe it was because of his recurring war wound, which is an on-going concern of his. Maybe he was injured at work. Well, what does he do for a living? He isn't a farmer: his two brothers are. I then said: "He's an attorney — an attorney who doesn't want to practice law." So, I made him a Lieutenant in the homicide squad for Belken County. And this, then, opened the doors for *Partners in Crime* which is also forthcoming from Arte Público Press. The novel deals with both Jehú and Rafa at their middle or later thirties. *Partners* is a part of *Klail City Death Trip* because it follows that bent I have for looking at society in general and making telling comments about it as time and the society change in Belken.

At present, I am working on something called *A Thief, A Liar, and a Murderer.* Once again, I'm bringing in the money from the banks which are the controlling interests everywhere. What I would like to do is to continue what I started in *Parters in Crime*; that is, to write about the false economy in the Valley; I speak of that economy which has been brought in by the drug trafficking down there. Drugs, in many ways, have transformed the Mexicano society in Belken; have broken up family units, for one; have destroyed a cohesiveness for another. . . .

José Saldívar: Rolando, besides being a novelist-poet, you are also an essayist-critic yourself. When you write fiction, do you lock the critic up, or does the critic-essayist-historian participate in the poetics of your work?

Rolando Hinojosa: I think that they all participate. I don't think I could ever write a novel without referring to some form of history. That much is evident when I first used a supposed diary from the Mexican Revolution as early as *Estampas*. That's just an example, but another one is the presentation of society, in historical terms, and this, too, appears as early as *Estampas*. The critic is always present; I think that if the writer isn't a critic, then he isn't much of a writer, or, not a serious writer. I also think that my work would be lacking without the presence of the historian, critic, and essayist in there.

José Saldívar: In many of your books, your texts seem to turn around an important issue that you cannot quite resolve to your satisfaction: namely, the relationship between Texas-Anglos and Texas-Mexicanos. Is your work about who gets the best of whom in that struggle? Is this too narrow a question?

Rolando Hinojosa: No, it isn't too narrow. It's an important point, too, but not the only one. You develop a psychological bond when you live close to someone; whether the Texas-Mexicano admits it or not, he is greatly influenced by this overwhelming culture and economy. But the Anglo, himself, whether he wants to admit it or not, is also greatly influenced by us in many ways. They too develop a strong psychological bond with us.

But, I won't paint a rosy picture. If we have scoundrels on the Anglo side, I'm going to bring them out. By the same token, what scoundrels there are on the Mexicano side should also be brought out. But, as far as resolving it, to use your term — because it's a very good term — I'm not even sure there *is* a resolution; therefore, it is dialectic. It has to continue.

José Saldívar: The next question is broad: In your essays "A Voice of One's Own," and "Chicano Literature: An American

Literature with a Difference," you allude to two very important figures in the literature of the Americas: José Martí and William Faulkner. What impact have Martí, Faulkner, and, let me add, García Márquez, had upon you and your work?

Rolando Hinojosa: When I was an undergraduate — as most undergraduates — I was assigned certain books. In my case, I was fortunate: I worked in the Reserved Reading Room at the library of the University of Texas for four years. I had a wider access to more books than most undergraduates.

The earliest piece I read by Martí was a brief prose assignment in some Spanish-American literature course. I was much taken by his writing and by the ideas he presented. One of the things he talked about was complete liberation and independence. I was also taken by the *way* he wrote and about what he termed Nuestra América, Our America. I also remember the report-essay on *el terremoto* in Charleston; that was a big influence, and I admit it freely. I could see the devastation in South Carolina because I had seen hurricane devastations in the Rio Grande Valley, where you and I are both from. The clarity of that writing also influenced me. I then steeped myself in the political tracts that he wrote when he was living in New York City and in other parts of the East Coast. Finally, his poetry attracted me as well. I thought it simple, unadorned, but I was wrong: it was strong and it has withstood in time, as has that lovely piece about the girl in Guatemala which I find effective still.

Eventually, I fell into Faulkner. Anyone who writes is going to have to read Faulkner. The first thing I read was a terrible thing called *Mosquitoes*. But when I read *The Unvanquished* — which in some ways parallels what I am doing with the Mexican Revolution in my work, as well as the coming together of different cultures here — I saw what I wanted to do later on. I reread *Mosquitoes* and from there went directly to *The Sound and The Fury* with its many points of view. This, too, has been a telling influence.

The influence I received from García Márquez is newspaper influence. I read more of his journalistic essays than anything else. The following is not a confession, it's an admission: I've never read *Cien años de soledad.* I would like to read it after I stop writing. I think that *Cien años* is such an overwhelming and important book that I am just going to have to let it go. I know of García Márquez's work certainly, and, yet, maybe Harold Bloom is right: it could be I have certain angst for contemporary writers.

For a person who hasn't read a single book or line by García Márquez, I certainly know a lot *about* him, and I most certainly appreciate what he has done. A brief example of something here: some reader told me that he or she, I think it was, saw a similarity between *"Al pozo con Bruno Cano"* in *Estampas* with *Los funerales de Mamá Grande* by García Márquez. I said I hadn't read the work; and I hadn't and haven't, but what else could I say?

José Saldívar: Enough anxiety of influence, for now. Let us turn to something more technical and ideological in your work, Rolando. When I teach the course on Chicano Literature at the University of Houston, we read Chicano fiction more generically than some of my students would like us to. For example, when we read Anaya's *Bless me, Ultima,* I follow Héctor Calderón's insight that Anaya's text, strictly speaking, is not a novel, but a romance. Now, it seems to me that your literary texts are generically encoded for your readers. *Mi querido Rafa,* of course, is essentially epistolary in genre. You claim that *Rites and Witnesses* is comedic in its structure, content, and ideology. Will you elaborate for us how *Rites and Witnesses* is a comedy?

Rolando Hinojosa: I will have to agree with you on the generic encoding of my work. I do, however, experiment a lot, because I think if other Mexicanos in the U.S. want to write, I want them to be free, and to feel free to write in any mode that they want. If they are well-read in the 18th century, particularly the British canon, then, they will understand that the epistolary genre is a tremendous on-going business at the time. The genre shouldn't die because it doesn't appear as often now; in passing, it's difficult to write because of its point of view.

I'm very interested in genre. Always have been. The romance, however, has never affected me much. I think I made that clear in *Klail City.*

To answer your question about *Rites and Witnesses,* I didn't know what to call it at first. As you know, a comedy doesn't have to be absurd or funny. *Rites and Witnesses* is a comedy of manners; it's not a comedy, such as Jane Austen's, though her language is biting at times. Mine may raise a welt or two; anyway, after the last re-write and re-read of *Rites,* I decided it *was* a comedy, and that was it.

José Saldívar: Rolando, I do not wish to end our conversation without discussing your presentation of women in *Klail City Death Trip.* To begin, let us recall what Joseph Sommers said about Tomás Rivera's *tierra*: that women in his book "tend to be presented either as passive prisoners of traditional culture in its most static form, or as tempters whose charms provoke men to tragedy." How do you represent women in your project? Could you say something about Viola Barragán, Marta, Sammie Jo, and other women?

Rolando Hinojosa: I haven't taken a census of the number of men and women in my books. I think that it is 60% men and 40% women. I put women in my work where I think it appropriate. If readers will read the life history of Viola Barragán in isolation, for instance, I think they will see that she is aggressive; there is nothing hypocritical about her — and hardly a temptress. Now, there's a void in my work because *Claros varones* isn't out and Viola is an axial character in it. She seems to be the strongest woman character that I have.

The role assigned to Marta in "Por esas cosas que pasan," is a recognizable role, given her lack of education, her brother's lack of education, and her husband's. The historical reasons for their lack of formal training is tacit. She, then, has to be the maintainer of the household in view of the fact that her mother is a paralytic. So, we have two paychecks coming into the house: her husband, Beto's, and her brother, Balde's. Marta is the one who keeps everything in line. No easy chore. She's no fool, either; she knows exactly what she's doing.

Other women, such as Doña Josefa, are also strong characters. She is the one who receives a letter from her husband in *Klail City*. He is fighting in the Mexican Revolution, and she is taking care of the household. Defending it, really. She's defeated, however, by the developers, as anyone would be defeated. But Doña Josefa maintains that particular household, and she's also responsible for the raising of some foundlings that were dropped off at her footstep.

I don't mean to pick on women. Most feminists don't even know my stance. To add to this, some critics are very selective as to what they are going to criticize — or to teach and emphasize in class. In this regard, I say to . . . my readers: Go back and reread; form your own opinions without outside influence.

José Saldívar: What about the ideology of racism in *Rites and Witnesses*?

Rolando Hinojosa: I wanted to present both men and women as racists because there are racists in both sexes. Some of them don't even know that they are racists. For instance, two of the women in *Rites and Witnesses*, one of them owns a camera shop, and the other one is a housewife, are both racists. One of them, if you'll recall, is very patronizing; the other one acts as if she were dispensing largesse. Both believe they are Southern gentry, acting out of benevolence when they hire Texas-Mexicanos to work for them at dirt wages.

José Saldívar: Can you comment about the psychology of your male characters?

Rolando Hinojosa: I'll talk about one trait, here. You have rascals in *Klail City Death Trip*, like Polín Tapia. Every time I write about Polín Tapia I burst out laughing: he is malleable, flexible, pliant. And the reason I also burst out laughing is because I see him as a Shakespearean rascal: a rogue, a two-suited slave, knave. When I first saw him as a coyote, hounding the halls of the Belken County courthouse — like Adrián Peralta — I said, this man is going to have to reappear again and again. He's a dynamic character. I don't want him to be *un tipo*; I really want him to be a persona. Remember that scene in *Rites and Witnesses* when he is on his way to see Noddy for that horrible political conference? Why, it's the most . . . Well, I'm glad I'm not Polín Tapia.

José Saldívar: Rolando, let us end on a local and ironic note. March 1984 has been designated Texas book month and Governor Mark White has issued a proclamation to that effect. We both know that there are hundreds of books by and about Texans to choose from. A. C. Greene, for instance, gives us fifty in his book, *50 Best Texas Books*. Were you surprised by your exclusion?

Rolando Hinojosa: No, not a bit.

José Saldívar: Could you give your ten best Texas books?

Rolando Hinojosa: I can't, because I don't keep them on the top of my head. One of the best Texas books of the 1970's is Tomás Rivera's . . . *y no se lo tragó la tierra,* which is not included in Mr. Greene's list. Tomás's book is a thin one, but it's like a steel girder. It will outlive the nonbooks written by some Texans in Greene's list — many of whom are professional Texans. Twenty years from now, Tomás Rivera's book will still be read; it's being read now, thirteen years after its publication, and *that's* a statement.

As for Governor White's pronouncement, well, I'm glad he's espousing book reading.

Let me conclude, José, by telling you what I do here at the University of Texas. As you know, I teach Chicano Literature in the undergraduate and graduate levels. However, my colleague Don Graham and I also teach *Life and Literature of the Southwest.*

When I came here three years ago, I decided that if we were going to teach a literature of the Southwest, we were going to have to include Américo Paredes, Tomás Rivera, myself, and others. So, aside from Sessions Perry, Gipson, and McMurtry, our students also read Paredes, Rivera, and me. This year we're reading *The Valley* and an urban novel, Willey's *November 22,* in addition to the others. Now, without the presence of the Texas-

Mexican in Southwest Literature, how can you teach a course of U.S. Southwest lit.? You can't. Life and literature cannot be exclusive; they have to be inclusive. This, after all, is Our Southwest, *nuestro suroeste.*